THE PENGUIN CLASSICS

EDITED BY E. V. RIEU

L97

DESCARTES

Discourse on Method

AND OTHER WRITINGS

*

*Translated with an Introduction
by Arthur Wollaston*

PENGUIN BOOKS

Penguin Books Ltd, Harmondsworth, Middlesex

U.S.A.: Penguin Books Inc., 3300 Clipper Mill Road, Baltimore 11, Md

AUSTRALIA: Penguin Books Pty Ltd, 762 Whitehorse Road,
Mitcham, Victoria

—

First published 1960

—

Made and printed in Great Britain
by The Whitefriars Press Ltd
London and Tonbridge

Contents

Introduction

I

DESCARTES is often called the founder of modern philosophy, and the statement contains a solid core of historical truth. But generalizations of this kind tend to suggest more than they really mean, and it seems best to begin with an attempt to characterize the philosophy of Descartes as a whole.

Descartes himself would no doubt have welcomed the title bestowed upon him by most historians of philosophy as signifying what he had intended from the start. He was, in fact, disposed to claim for his philosophy an absolute beginning, to see in his achievement, as Bertrand Russell has said in his *History of Western Philosophy*, a self-centred, and self-sufficient philosophical edifice, established on original foundations, and owing nothing to any other architect or builder. And his family circumstances were such as to encourage him in this attitude. His first biographer, the Abbé Baillet, made an attempt to establish a claim to noble birth for his hero, but there seems to be no very good reason for accepting this claim. The fact is that Descartes came of what we should now call a well-to-do professional family, and that there was nothing exalted about his heredity or his circumstances, just as there was nothing to suggest his future greatness. His father, indeed, a councillor in the Parliament of Brittany, looked askance at what he called his son's propensity for 'having himself bound in calf', that is, for publishing tomes of philosophy; but the family was wealthy, and René Descartes' share in the family fortunes was sufficient, although he was the younger son, to keep him in moderate affluence all his life, and to leave him free to pursue his vocation as a philosopher – philosophy itself being, in the definition accepted by Descartes, the pursuit of wisdom. The competence which Descartes enjoyed was inadequate, as he frequently complains, to cover the cost of all the experiments he needed to make in order to renew, as he hoped to do, the whole of human knowledge; but it was adequate to free him from the

necessity, as he puts it in the *Discourse on Method*, of making a
'trade of his knowledge'. Thus, in a world of University
doctors, that is to say, of professional philosophers, Descartes
was an amateur with private means. And the fact has its
importance; it helped to preserve his cherished independence
as a thinker.

Nevertheless, Descartes was much more a man of his time,
much more exposed to the mental climate of his day, than he
no doubt realized himself. Born on 31 March 1596, in the
little village of La Haye, now called Descartes-La-Haye, in
Touraine, Descartes belongs to the last phase of the Renaissance. By the time he reached early manhood, eighty years
had elapsed since the discovery of the true system of the
universe; pure mathematics had been enriched by the invention of symbolic algebra and logarithms; while Tycho Brahé,
Kepler, Galileo, and others had made their own discoveries.
And all this had been achieved by the new devotion to mathematics. It soon appeared to Descartes, gazing with distaste on
the decadent scholastic philosophy and science of his time –
and science and philosophy were never separated in his
mind – that the same highly successful mathematical method
could have a wider range, that it would in fact be extended to
philosophy as a whole – which for Descartes meant the whole
of rational knowledge. For, he observes, 'only the mathematicians have been able to find any demonstrations, that is,
any certain and evident reasons.' Hence his conclusion, 'not
indeed that arithmetic and geometry are the only sciences to
be studied, but merely that in our search for the direct road
to truth we should busy ourselves with no object about which
we cannot attain a certainty equal to that of the demonstrations
of arithmetic and geometry.' The aim of Descartes, therefore,
was not to give a mathematical interpretation of the universe,
but to compose a philosophy in the likeness of mathematics,
to exhibit all varieties of knowledge as the consequence of a
set of ultimate principles of final simplicity which would be
universally accepted like mathematical axioms. Thus the
essential part of the philosopher's task would be done, and
philosophy would have attained the certainty of mathematics.
The rest would consist in the drawing out of further con-

sequences in the form of fresh discoveries in the whole domain of knowledge, which might give room for controversy over details, but not for fundamental disagreement.

Thus the first characteristic of Descartes' thought is his mathematical, or quasi-mathematical, view of the conditions of knowledge, and we have seen how his universal *mathesis* – as he called it – was inspired. Again, it was his avowed purpose to be rid once and for all of Aristotle and his sectaries, as he calls them, to be rid, that is to say, of Scholasticism. Now, ever since the fourteenth century, men had been found to criticize Aristotle; the ambition of Descartes was different, it was to replace him. Nevertheless, he retains and uses for his own purposes a number of Scholastic notions. He has no doubt about 'substance', which he regards as a fundamental idea requiring no further explanation; he accepts the later Scholastic division of being into formal or actual being – real existence – and objective being,[1] or the existence of ideas in the mind, just as he accepts the Scholastic notion of degrees of reality or perfection,[1] so that the idea of God must have more 'objective' reality in the mind than any other idea, and must have for its adequate cause God Himself, the supremely actual, or real, Being. Similarly, while he rejects the Aristotelian doctrine of form and matter, and reduces all causality in effect to the efficient cause, sweeping aside final causes in particular, his views of causality in general, of the finite and the infinite, are substantially the same as those of the Scholastics. We are still some way from Hume.

And yet, when all this has been said, it remains true that Descartes was not entirely mistaken in his opinion of what he undoubtedly regarded as his mission – his mission as a philosopher; nor was Hegel at fault in calling him 'the grand initiator of modern thought'. The mission of Descartes was not simply to do battle with Aristotle, and to reduce all causality to the efficient cause. Coming at the end of the Renaissance, his philosophy is largely an attempt to sum up and to satisfy what seem to have been the twin aspirations of the Renaissance mind: the establishment of a fully autonomous form of knowledge – the noblest, says Descartes, in the first

1. See Note on Cartesian Terminology, pp. 191, 192.

of the works translated in this volume, the *Discourse on Method*, of 'the purely human occupations of men'; and the assignment to this knowledge of the task of going beyond the contemplation of its object to the possession and use of this object for the general amelioration and increase of human life – so that we may become, as Descartes says, also in the *Discourse*, 'the lords and masters of nature'. Thus in the last of the three pieces translated here, in the *Letter-Preface* to his *Principles of Philosophy*, Descartes compares 'the whole of philosophy to a tree of which the aphysics forms the roots, and physics the trunk, while the branches which grow from this trunk constitute all the other sciences which may be reduced to three: medicine, mechanics, and ethics ...' Metaphysics no longer ends in contemplation, but serves as the ground for that knowledge of nature from which spring all the sciences that minister to our well-being.

Two further points should be noted to complete these preliminary remarks on the philosophy of Descartes. After the decadence of medieval thought and the vagaries of Renaissance speculation, he was the first philosopher to construct a coherent system of ideas, and to open up a new way of thinking in place of the prevalent confusion; and he was also the first to draw the attention of philosophers to the problem of certainty as such. It is for this perhaps that Descartes is now chiefly remembered, and it arose from his conception in conformity with Renaissance aspirations, of what philosophy should be – an autonomous form of knowledge. But how can knowledge be autonomous, in the full sense of the term, unless it has an absolute beginning, and how can it have an absolute beginning, unless that beginning is self-assured, carrying with it, so to speak, its own credentials of truth? In his *The Problem of Knowledge*, Professor Ayer remarks, 'I conclude then that the necessary and sufficient conditions for knowing that something is the case are first that what is said is known to be true, secondly that one can be sure of it, and thirdly that one should have the right to be sure.' It is the third of these conditions that particularly exercised Descartes, and which he rightly thought indispensable at the outset of the sort of philosophy he was seeking. Besides, in the general disarray of thought, scepticism seemed the safest attitude to adopt: Montaigne is the great exemplar. It was necessary, Descartes thought, to put an end to this scepticism before the human mind could make any real progress. Hence the problem of certainty was central in his thought, as it has been in philosophy ever since.

2

The first step in Descartes' intellectual itinerary in his quest for certainty came early – as soon, he tells us in the first part of the *Discourse*, as he had completed the course of studies which constituted his formal education. It was the rejection as infected with doubt and uncertainty of all – or of almost all – that was considered knowledge or learning in his time. He had been sent at an early age to the celebrated Jesuit College of La Flèche, recently founded by Henri IV, where he was an eager and brilliant pupil, and where his enlightened schoolmasters kindly allowed him to lie late in bed in the mornings, not so much because he was delicate and needed more sleep than other boys as because that was the time and the manner in which his mind worked best. The privileged hours were spent by the young Descartes in mental effort, not sleep; and the habit remained with him all his life. Then, after he had left La Flèche at the age of sixteen and had taken a degree in Law at the University of Poitiers, there happened to him what happens to many young men at the end of their scholastic careers – he realized that he knew nothing. But with Descartes the reason was not that he had been unable or unwilling to learn anything; it was that everything he had learned seemed to him in the end nothing. 'For,' he writes in the *Discourse*, 'I found myself hampered by so many doubts and errors that my efforts to learn seemed to have had no other effect than to make me increasingly aware of my own ignorance.'

It is of course a good thing to become aware of one's own ignorance, but Descartes meant that he had become suspicious of all knowledge. Others had come to the same conclusion, for varying reasons, before Descartes; Montaigne, for instance, whose account of his own schooldays seems to anticipate that of Descartes. Horrified by the religious and political quarrels of his time and by the disruption of European unity consequent upon the Reformation, Montaigne discovered the source of all these evils in dogmatism. Men are so infatuated by their own beliefs that they will not hesitate to kill an opponent, as if ridding him of his life were to rid the world of his opinions. But true wisdom consists in a careful training of the mind to suspend judgement: that is the final lesson of the *Essays*. A good mind is never irrevocably bound to its own opinions; it is assured neither of its knowledge, nor even, one may perhaps add, of its ignorance. It will assert neither 'I know', nor 'I don't know', but only ask 'What do I know?' That is the mark of wisdom.

Almost every page of the *Discourse* bears witness to the care with which Descartes had read the *Essays*. Even the first words of the *Discourse* are an echo of a sentence in Montaigne's *Essay on Presumption*. But what was the conclusion for Montaigne was only a starting-point for Descartes. If his education had turned him into something of a sceptic, his scepticism was provisional; he was a sceptic hoping for something better than scepticism.

The *Discourse on Method* marks a turning-point in the history of European thought, but it is by no means the formal treatise which its title suggests. Published in 1637, and composed in the easy French of a seventeenth-century gentleman, it was addressed to readers of the same stamp, and its appeal to the ordinary cultivated man and woman was enhanced by a narrative of high personal interest. Descartes' first intention had been to call it 'A History of my Mind', and it may still be read as such, whatever we may think of the validity of Descartes' philosophy as a whole. The *Discourse on Method* is therefore, in the first place, a sort of memoir, and a memoir is always a revival of the past in the light of the present. When Descartes left La Flèche, we may suppose that his ideas were not as definite as they appear to be some twenty years later in the *Discourse* itself. Nevertheless, the past contains the seeds of the present, and a man who writes the history of his thoughts, knowing himself, as he does, from within, has the right to stress their continuity. No doubt Descartes' scepticism at the end of his schooldays was less thoroughgoing than the *Discourse* suggests; mathematics was in any case exempted from the general condemnation; but it is safe to say that he left La Flèche with a feeling of profound dissatisfaction, half conscious perhaps of what I have called his mission, and determined meanwhile to abandon book learning, and to seek for knowledge, first in 'the great book of the world', and then in himself.

We find him, accordingly, after a period of travel about which we know very little, and which is only alluded to in the *Discourse*, engaged as a gentleman volunteer in the army of Prince Maurice of Nassau, in Holland. War was a leisurely business in those happy days, and Descartes occupied his abundant leisure in learning Dutch, and in the study of applied sciences, such as military architecture and the theory of music. A chance encounter with a young Dutchman, Isaac Beeckman, a few years older than himself, recalled him to his true vocation. For Beeckman recognized in Descartes a man after his own heart, one of those physico-mathematicians, as he calls them, whose paucity he bemoans in his journal. From this journal, and from the correspondence which sprang up between the two new friends, we can see how Beeckman's questions directed Descartes' attention towards just those theoretical problems with which his genius was best fitted to deal. Their meeting took place in November 1618; by the following March Descartes could write to Beeckman that he had just discovered four demonstrations in geometry, all of them important, and all entirely new. And then followed a bold generalization characteristic of the eager process of his thought: if he could solve four problems, why should it not be possible to find a more general method which could be applied to all geometrical problems whatsoever? It was an immense task for a young man barely twenty-three years of age, but Descartes had some confidence that he might achieve it. 'My project,' he writes to Beeckman, 'is incredibly ambitious, but I cannot help feeling that I have caught a glimmer of I know not what light in the chaos of present-day geometry, and I trust that it will help me to dispel that most opaque darkness.'

Descartes was on the track of what was to become analytical geometry, and when exactly the full light of his discovery shone upon him we do not know. Meanwhile he had left Holland and was on his way into Germany to take service with the Emperor Maximilian whose coronation he had just witnessed. But the Emperor's army had gone into winterquarters, and Descartes himself settled down in a little village near Ulm, where, he writes, having no society to distract him, and no cares or passions to disturb him, he spent a whole day shut up alone in a stove-heated room with complete leisure to occupy himself with his own thoughts. What these were he tells us in studiously moderate language in this second part of the *Discourse*. But the *Discourse*, it must be remembered, was written seventeen years later, when, as a man of forty and a philosopher, he was more concerned with the long train of reflections by which he sought to justify his philosophical position than with the dramatic character of the underlying experience. At the time he was, he wrote in a personal note, '*rempli d'enthousiasme*', 'brimming over with inspiration'. And that same night, the night of 10 November 1619, he was visited by dreams, which seemed to him to have been sent to him by God, and in which he ventured to find a confirmation of the thoughts with which he had been agitated all day.

He was, as we know, at least on the verge of an epochmaking discovery in mathematics. According to his own interpretation of his dreams, Descartes proceeded immediately, and in characteristic fashion, to an even wider generalization. If two sciences, hitherto regarded as distinct, could be shown to be one, why should it not be possible to show that all the sciences are one, to find a universal method of solving all the problems with which the human mind is confronted, whatever the branch of knowledge concerned, provided only that they be mathematical problems, or can be dealt with on a mathematical model? Furthermore, the discovery and use of such a method can only be the work of one man from its very nature, and he himself was that man, for he was the only one who knew what the restoration of the human mind from its actual state of doubt and uncertainty required and could thus discover the key to the rational explanation of reality. One of the first considerations that occurred to him in the stove-heated room, says Descartes, was that there is often less perfection in works 'carried out by various masters than in those on which a single individual has laboured'. Thus the first step was the combination of two mathematical sciences; the second, the combination of logic and mathematics; and the whole was to be achieved by a single mind.

This was Descarte's final illumination, the basic vision at the age of twenty-three, so discreetly exploited – if the term may be allowed – in the *Discourse on Method*, from which emerged not only the *Discourse* but the whole Cartesian philosophy. And from then onwards, Descartes, now fully conscious of his mission, could see his way clear before him. Still too young, as he admits in the *Discourse*, to set out immediately upon his grandiose enterprise, he decided to spend the next few years in preparing himself for his task by trying out his method on a variety of subjects including geometry. Next he would start on the building of the whole edifice of the sciences, and, by the time of his death, the whole business would be complete.

The period of apprenticeship lasted nine years, during which Descartes did nothing but study particular questions, especially in mathematics and physics. Then, feeling that his project was sufficiently precise in his mind, he returned to Holland in 1628, not, as has often been stated, without any real evidence, in order to escape possible persecution by the absolute government of Louis XIII, but for the sake of the solitude and the freedom from importunate friends which he found indispensable for his work. The first nine months he spent, as we learn later from his correspondence, in the composition of a 'little treatise on divinity', now lost, but of which the substance was no doubt incorporated in the *Meditations on the First Philosophy* (the second of the works translated in this volume) and published thirteen years later. He also attempted to codify in his *Rules for the Direction of the Mind* (published after his death) those notions on method which came to his mind as he worked on various scientific problems. But his main preoccupation till the publication of the *Discourse* (which replaced the *Rules* for Descartes) in 1637 was the working out of his conception of the physical universe in a book to which he refers as his 'world'. Descartes worked slowly; his was one of those rare minds that prefer thinking to writing; few thinkers have been less ambitious of the title of author. The 'world' was to be in two parts, the first devoted to physical theory, and the second to anatomy as the basis of medicine, which Descartes regarded as the most beneficial of the sciences. And as all the sciences were one, the same mathematical or quasi-mathematical method must apply to medicine as well as physics. We see an example of this in Descartes' attempt in the fifth chapter of the *Discourse* at once to defend and correct Harvey's explanation of the circulation of the blood. However, the first part of the 'World' had been barely completed when the condemnation of Galileo for having maintained the movement of the earth caused him to lay aside his work, of which the same hypothesis was in reality an integral part.

Descartes' behaviour on this occasion has been put down to pusillanimity; it would be not only more charitable but more accurate to ascribe it to prudence. Uncompromising as he might be in holding to the truth as he saw it, Descartes was always most circumspect in putting forward his views. His aim was to be accepted as an authority in the place of Aristotle, and he had no desire to frighten away the ignorant or to alienate the conservative. Galileo, he was sure, had been condemned on a misunderstanding. He had no desire to suffer a similar fate, and so his philosophical activity during the next few years was at least partly inspired by the desire to create an atmosphere favourable to his views, in which any such misunderstanding would be impossible. If he could show that by the method which he employed in the explanation of the physical universe, and which had brought him to the discovery of analytical geometry, he also possessed a philosophy 'more certain than the common one' which included proofs, as convincing as those of mathematics, of the existence of God, and of the nature of the human soul, theologians and philosophers might unite in acclaiming him and even in begging him to publish his 'world'. Hence, in the first place, the publication of the *Discourse* as a preface to two scientific essays, and one mathematical one: the first on meteors, the second on dioptrics, and the third on geometry. The first two essays were to serve as examples of Descartes' new way of dealing with the explanation of physical phenomena, while the fifth part of the *Discourse* itself includes a general account of the physical theories he would have expounded in full detail in his 'World'. The third essay, Descartes tells us, was meant to encourage others in the search for truth by showing that there were still new truths to be discovered.

The essays, like the *Discourse*, were written in French, and the educated lay public for whom the whole volume was primarily intended responded heartily; but academic circles, in particular Descartes' old masters, the Jesuits, whose approbation he felt would have won him the battle, remained obdurate in their rejection of his anti-Aristotelianism, and Descartes next attempted to establish his position by the publication in 1641, four years after the *Discourse*, of his *Meditations*, of which the full title of the second edition is eloquent of his intentions: *Meditations on the First Philosophy in which the Existence of God and the Real Distinction of Mind and Body are Demonstrated*. What we may call official approval was still withheld, however, despite the fact that the *Meditations* were originally written in Latin and published with a dedication to the Theological Faculty of the Sorbonne, and Descartes found himself the object on all sides of critical attacks. Nevertheless, it is the *Meditations* which contain the full exposition of Descartes' doctrine on 'first philosophy' or metaphysics, and we may now turn to a consideration of his argument in this respect.

3

For Descartes, as we have seen, the central problem was the problem of certainty; it had been forced upon him, as we have also seen, almost as soon as he had left school, and the general purpose of the *Discourse on Method* was to show how he had himself encountered the problem and dealt with it. How can we be sure of knowing anything? For Montaigne there was no answer to this question; the note of interrogation was a note of finality, a full-stop, and true wisdom consisted in accepting this state of affairs, and in resting one's head comfortably on the 'soft pillow' of scepticism. But to Descartes such a posture was profoundly unsatisfactory. True wisdom does not arise from erudition, from a prolonged commerce with the writings of others, as Montaigne's practice suggested, but from the perfection and consequent satisfaction of the mind. There are degrees of wisdom, Descartes says in the *Letter-Preface* to his *Principles of Philosophy*, and the highest consists in the discovery of 'the first causes and true principles from which everything we are capable of knowing may be deduced'. Nor did he regard the task as a super-human one; it was, he thought, within the capacity of anyone whose mind had not been hopelessly distorted by the errors and prejudices of his education, or corrupted by his own laziness and indifference to the highest wisdom. All that was required was an unprejudiced mind which should follow what Descartes calls its natural light. For we all have this light and in the same degree; that is the meaning of the opening sentences of the *Discourse*, and that is the ultimate significance of the Cartesian Method that it allows us to follow this natural light by acting as a sort of therapeutic of the mind and freeing us from all forms of error.

Thus when Descartes set out, in the *Meditations*, to construct the new philosophy, of which the fourth part of the *Discourse* gives an outline, and which was to replace the old, outworn, and uncertain Scholastic philosophy, he realized that his search was for the fundamental notions on which all know-ledge rests and which are immediately evident to an attentive mind unclouded by error and prejudice. As a mathematician, and in order to make the objects of philosophical knowledge as similar to the axioms of mathematics as possible, he reduced the number of these fundamental notions to three: thought, God, and extension in length, breadth, and depth; and the line of his argument always runs from the thinking self to God, and from God to the external world. As a mathematician, again, the process of Descartes' thought is commanded by a mathematician's conception of the nature and function of ideas.

Descartes' mathematicism is implicit rather than explicit in his exposition of his doctrine. The *Meditations* are in fact the 'little treatise on divinity' which Descartes composed immediately upon return to Holland in 1628, and their subject is the existence of God and of the soul. But the point to emphasize is that in the new philosophy of Descartes, unlike the old philosophy of Aristotle, the movement of thought is from ideas to things, and not from things to ideas. What is a triangle to a mathematician? It is not of course the triangle I can construct roughly out of three bits of sticks, or even draw more precisely on a piece of paper or on the blackboard; it is the definition of a triangle which gives its essence, and nothing else. It may even be that no such thing as a triangle has ever existed in reality; but that is a matter of indifference to the mathematician as such who is interested simply in the essence of the triangle as contained in its definition. Similarly for Descartes the most important ideas are innate ideas, which he finds in his mind – 'those', he says, 'that are born with me', which he perceives 'clearly and distinctly', and which are like images or pictures of the reality they represent. Hence the principle implicit not only in Cartesianism but in the whole body of modern idealism: all that can be known *clearly* and *distinctly* as constituting the idea of a thing may be said of the thing itself; there is no opaque residue to defeat the intellect as in the Aristotelian conception of matter and form.

Descartes hardly treats the difference between 'clear' and 'distinct' formally, but we have only to consider the notion of, for instance, a triangle, neglecting the visual image, and paying attention only to its essence, to understand what is meant by calling an idea *clear*. The same idea is called *distinct* because it is exclusive. When the mathematician contemplates one or other of the objects of his thought, he not only knows what it is, but also what it is not. A circle is a circle because it has the properties of a circle, and none of those that make a triangle; while, on the contrary, we are left in doubt as to whether heat is the absence of cold, or cold the absence of heat, so that these are obscure and confused ideas in which we can have no confidence. Thus the proper procedure of the philosopher who has a correct understanding of the mathematical method in philosophy is to move not only from thought to existence, but from clear and distinct existences. 'When we say that something is contained in the nature or concept of anything, that is precisely the same as saying that it is true of the thing or can be affirmed of it.' But when we touch some material thing, and find it hot or cold, we cannot say, as the Scholastics did, that it has the property of heat or the property of cold, for these ideas are neither clear nor distinct.

Such was the conception of knowledge underlying the philosophy of Descartes. We should be able to construct the world out of our clear and distinct ideas, certain that these ideas will constitute a true picture of the reality, and the problem then is the problem of finding the right order in which to set out the ideas we find in our minds, and of making more, as Descartes suggests at the opening of the fourth part of the *Discourse*, of our starting-point so that it may be proof against all the criticisms of the sceptics. Now the first of the four rules laid down in the *Discourse* for the proper conduct of the mind is: To accept as true nothing I did not know to be evidently so. And the second rule: To divide each difficulty into as many parts as would be required the better to solve it. But if we take these two rules together, what is the first question that must be answered? It is the question Descartes asks in the first *Meditation*, whether there is anything at all that can be evidently known. And the answer had to be, not in the realm of abstract mathematical thought, but in the order of existence, yet still mathematical, so to speak, in spirit, so as to provide that initial self-sufficing axiom with which Renaissance thinking, and Descartes himself, aspired to begin, if philosophy were to be truly autonomous.

In other words, Descartes had to find an existential proposition of an Euclidean simplicity and infallibility that would withstand the most extravagant objections of the sceptics; and he found it, as everybody knows, in the celebrated *cogito ergo sum*, 'I think, therefore I am'. For let me institute what Descartes calls a methodic doubt; let me outbid even Montaigne in the practice of scepticism; let me not only impugn the testimony of the senses, point to the normal fallibility of the human mind, fail to distinguish clearly between my dreams and my waking-moments, but let me also suppose that there is no God but a malicious Demon whose wicked and ingenious pleasure it is systematically to deceive me about everything my mind cannot help accepting as true – even then I can say, as Descartes does in the second *Meditation*, 'But there is no doubt that I exist in being deceived, and so, let him deceive me as much as he likes, he can never turn me into nothing so long as I think that I am something.' Doubt, it seems, could go no further; Descartes called it *hyperbolical*, and was sure that he had drawn from it the first of those 'true principles', as he says in the *Letter-Preface*, 'from which may be deduced the reasons of everything that can be known'. A principle, that is to say, not in the Aristotelian sense of an abstract and universally valid statement, but in the new Cartesian sense of a beginning or starting-point for the acquisition of real knowledge.

Stern logicians, including Bertrand Russell, have suggested that Descartes' proposition is invalid: the utmost he could say was not *I think, therefore I am*, but only *There is thought*. But, leaving aside the question as to what we can possibly mean by thought without a thinker, this is to misunderstand what Descartes, at least, considered he had proved. The *cogito ergo sum* is the affirmation not of the self and of thought taken separately as subject and verb, but of a thinking self taken as a whole – of an existence whose 'whole nature or essence', as he expresses it elsewhere, 'consists in thinking'. Thus I know that I exist, and I perceive the fact clearly and distinctly, I have a clear and distinct perception of myself as what Descartes later calls a 'thinking thing'.[1] I can dispel any doubts, even the doubt inspired by the hypothesis of a malicious Demon, since to be deceived is a form of thinking even though it be thinking erroneously; and, at the same time, I can understand what makes something true. I know that I exist because I perceive the fact clearly and distinctly. It follows that I am justified in asserting that whatever can be conceived clearly and distinctly in the mind is thereby true,

1. See Note on Cartesian Terminology, p. 192.

and the truth of the *cogito* becomes the exemplar of all other truths, and the secure starting-point of Descartes' philosophy.

More than three centuries separate us from the formulation of the *cogito* in the fourth part of the *Discourse* and in the *Meditations*, and yet we can still, I think, understand Descartes' doctrine as he understood it himself. The philosophical process begins with an initial intuition, from which other intuitions flow by a rigorous deduction. Then comes an immense effort to transcend deduction itself by reintegrating its successive stages in a comprehensive vision of the whole body of human knowledge grounded on the truth of its first principle and sharing in the light of its evidence. Is this not mathematical certitude? Descartes at least thought it was. The fourth and last rule of method, says Descartes, is 'to make so complete an enumeration of the links in an argument, and to pass them all so thoroughly under review, that I could be sure I had missed nothing'. This is the very essence of the Cartesian philosophy.

But let us turn to the Cartesian proofs of the existence of God, which follow directly upon the *cogito*. The *cogito* in itself only allows me to affirm my own existence; but if I can say, *I think, therefore I am*, I can also say, *I doubt, therefore I am*, since doubting, like being deceived, is a form of thinking; and further, if I consider the matter attentively, I can add to Descartes' statement and say, *I doubt, therefore God exists*. Nor is this so much of a paradox as it seems. For to doubt is to be imperfect, and I thus know what imperfection means. But how can I know this, how can I know that I am imperfect, unless I have the idea of perfection[1] clearly and distinctly in my mind? And what is this idea which implies in the philosophical vocabulary of Descartes' day the summit of reality or being, the *ens realissimum* of the Scholastics, but the idea of God? Now it is not very difficult to prove that an actually existing God is the only conceivable cause of this idea; for everything must have a cause, and the cause must be adequate to its effect. Only God Himself could be the cause of my idea of Him.

This is Descartes' first proof, a proof from efficient

1. See Note on Cartesian Terminology, p. 191.

causality, of the existence of God, and the whole argument is set out fully in the third *Meditation*. The next step was to prove the existence of other beings, if any such existed, for so far Descartes is sure only of his own existence, as what he calls a 'thinking thing', and of the existence of God; but he stops, at this stage, in the fifth *Meditation*, to expound a second proof of the existence of God inspired by his knowledge of geometrical proofs and definitions. This is Descartes' famous ontological proof of the existence of God, and his argument requires to be carefully followed, for it has often been misunderstood. We live so much in our senses that we are inclined to neglect the idea of God we have in our minds, or even to deny His existence; but if we become attentive to this idea, we see at once that it involves the real existence of God, just as when we conceive a triangle in our minds we see at once that our idea of the triangle involves all its necessary properties. In the same way our idea of God involves His existence. For what could we mean by a non-existent perfection? If it does not exist it is not perfection. We are no more free to think of God as non-existent than we are free to think of a sphere of which the circumference is not equidistant from the centre. Existence belongs to God as necessarily as the properties of a geometrical figure belong to that figure. Thus Descartes was able to write to his chief correspondent, the Oratorian priest, Mersenne, just after he had composed his 'little treatise on divinity': 'As for me I dare to boast of having found a proof of God's existence which I find fully satisfactory and by which I know that God exists more certainly than I know the truth of any geometrical proposition.' And what Descartes meant was not simply that he had proved the existence of a First Cause, but that he had proved that that First Cause was God, the Perfect Being. Thus, as the Perfect Being cannot deceive us, and as we have proved His existence, we can laugh at all our previous doubts, in particular we are liberated from the hypothesis of a malicious Demon; we can trust our good sense or reason and rely upon those clear and distinct ideas which are revealed to us by the natural light of our minds, secure in the veracity of the Perfect Being. For 'the certitude and truth of all science depend upon the knowledge of God and upon that alone ... (and) the certitude of all other truths is dependent on this one, that without the knowledge of God it would be impossible to know anything else.' It is in this sense that Descartes regards the idea of God as anterior to all other ideas.

The *cogito* leads to the proofs of the existence of God as the Sovereign Perfection; it had already given Descartes a clear idea of his own existence as a 'thinking thing', and a 'thinking thing' is a 'thing which doubts, understands, conceives, affirms, denies, wills, and does not will, which also imagines and feels'. He therefore knew what he was and by the same token he knew what he was not; for a clear idea is at the same time a distinct idea. Aristotle and his followers had explained the world in terms of matter and form, and attributed to the human body a soul or animating form which exercised various operations in and through the body such as nutrition, motion, sensation, and so on. But what we call the soul is, in Descartes' view, essentially thought, and the idea of the body is in no way contained within the clear idea of thought; it must therefore be excluded from it, if we want it also to be a distinct idea. It follows that, as the idea of the soul or mind contains nothing pertaining to a body, the soul itself is radically separate from the body, on the principle that distinct ideas are representative of distinct existences. Hence the famous or notorious Cartesian dualism of mind and matter, body and soul, that 'bifurcation of nature', as Whitehead called it, which has so deeply affected the course of European philosophy. The philosopher, when he deals with metaphysics, might as well forget that he has a body, just as the physicist as such can safely neglect his soul. And, when we ask what we mean by the body or, more generally matter, the answer is clear, once we have emancipated ourselves from the Aristotelian doctrine of matter and form, which is in effect nothing more than a disguised animism. We have only to inspect the idea of matter to see that it is pure extension in space according to the three dimensions; and we can now see clearly what Pascal meant by his saying that Descartes made his *cogito* the firm basis of an entire physics. Metaphysics is a pure spiritualism, which opens the way to a thoroughgoing mathematical interpretation of the physical universe, and which at the same time guarantees that interpretation; and it is on these three notions of thought, God, and extension, as I have already said, that Descartes constructs the whole edifice of his doctrine.

4

Thus did Descartes make his metaphysics the roots of the tree of which physics is the trunk, and a great deal of ink has been spilt on the question as to which came first in his own estimation, the trunk or the roots, his physics or his metaphysics. The answer is partly that Descartes did not distinguish between the two as sharply as we do today. By making his physics depend upon his metaphysics Descartes reversed the traditional procedure whereby the former constituted a sort of prolegomenon to the latter, as we see in the philosophy of Aristotle and of Aquinas; but he was even more convinced than most Scholastic thinkers of the need for continuity between the two. The term philosophy meant for him what we now call science as well as what we call philosophy; hence his picture of the tree of knowledge as a single whole. Indeed Aquinas seems to show a clearer anticipation of the modern view of the distinction between science and philosophy when he observes that the Ptolemaic theory of epicycles may 'save the appearances', but that that is not sufficient proof that the theory is true, 'for the appearances might perhaps also be saved on another hypothesis.'

The vogue of Cartesian physics lasted more than a generation. About the middle of the seventeenth century, a few years before Descartes' death, the learned Father Daniel of the Company of Jesus, in an amusing and often discerning satire, entitled *Voyage du Monde de M. Descartes*, could write (in the language of his contemporary English translator):

As in Spain the name of Lutheran is indifferently given to all Hereticks of whatever sect or fashion, so the title of Cartesian is attributed to all those that have undertaken since your day to make Refinements in point of Natural Philosophy.

Such a tribute coming from an opponent is striking; but

thirty years later it was a different story. As soon as Newton had published his *Mathematical Principles of Natural Philosophy* in 1687, it was clear that the Cartesian system of the physical universe was a thing of the past, at least among serious scientists. When, about the year 1732, Voltaire became a convert to Newton's physics, as he records in his *Lettres philosophiques*, educated opinion in France followed him, and few, if any, of the physical laws formulated by Descartes have been held as valid by scientists since that time.

On the other hand Descartes, though he remained unaware of the modern notion of a scientific hypothesis and, indeed, would have rejected it, since one implication of his philosophy is that there is no such thing as corrigible knowledge, did succeed in defining in a manner which has hardly been modified the object of physical science. The great merit of his metaphysics in his eyes was that it established the ground for a proper understanding of the physical universe, for the great enterprise which, as he says in the *Discourse*, will make us 'lords and masters of nature'. God guarantees the veracity of our ideas, provided only we conceive them clearly and distinctly, and the idea of extension shows us what the external world must be like: an odourless, colourless conglomeration of existents located in space and time. Others, Galileo for example, had conceived of the universe in the same way, but Descartes was the first to elaborate the conception, however erroneously, in detail, and above all, to make it part of a general philosophy. There are no Cartesians today in physics, but the problem of relating the new way of understanding the physical world to our knowledge of the world of the spirit is still with us. Descartes was the first fully to grasp this problem, and, even though we should be rash to accept his solution as final, we may still learn a great deal from it.

The Cartesian conception of the mind acting in magnificent independence of its body swept Europe. Leibniz in Germany, Malebranche in France, Spinoza in Holland; were all such minds who, in theory at least, felt no dependence on their bodies for the validity of their ideas. They all accepted the Cartesian theory of knowledge, and his mathematical conception of the process of the mind. But this radical dualism of mind and body is perhaps the basic difficulty in the Cartesian philosophy, and was soon noticed as such. Indeed, the attempts to overcome this dualism have filled the history of modern philosophy from Locke himself to Professor Gilbert Ryle, and lie at the roots of the quarrels between idealism and materialism, rationalism and empiricism, with which the student of philosophy is only too familiar.

For how on Descartes' principles do we know that we have bodies? The answer comes in the sixth and last *Meditation*. The idea of extension tells us what the external world is like for the mathematical physicist; but from the idea of extension we can deduce nothing about its existence as we can from the idea of God. Nor are the *images* of physical things any help; what we *imagine* cannot lead to the judgement that what we imagine, exists in fact. There remain our sensations of colour, heat, weight, and so on, which in the interests of mathematical physics Descartes regards – in modern terminology – as at least partly *subjective*, and having only a practical objectivity. They are, therefore, ideas, but unlike other ideas which are clear and distinct, they are confused and obscure, and therefore unreliable. They show, however, that the mind in forming these confused and obscure ideas has been affected by some alien substance intimately conjoined with it, and this substance is the body. Now each mind, being thus aware of its union with a body, also becomes aware of external action upon that body. It must consequently admit the existence of other bodies, and there can be no further doubt of the existence of the external world.

This proof satisfied Descartes, but, as might be expected, it satisfied hardly anyone else. At this stage, Leibniz remarks: 'M. Descartes threw in his hand.' No one hitherto had thought it necessary to prove the existence of matter, and, to judge by the subsequent controversies in philosophy, perhaps a good deal of trouble would have been avoided if the external world, like Caesar's wife, had remained above suspicion. But if Descartes thought his proof satisfactory, it was perhaps, because he did not realize its importance. His conception of philosophical knowledge is certainly the main source of the philosophy of idealism; Hegel was quite sure of this; but Descartes himself was not an idealist. He had no doubt that the clear and distinct ideas formed independently in the mind were representative, with the exactitude of mathematical definitions, of independent realities. The idea of extension was without doubt such an idea, even if its existence independently of the mind had, in a certain way, to be proved.

5

The *Meditations*, as I have said, failed to make any impression on academic circles, and in 1644 Descartes published *The Principles of Philosophy*, of which the first part was substantially a repetition of the metaphysical doctrine of the *Meditations* in a new form, while the rest contained his theory of the physical universe as a whole, what we may call his cosmology. But this new publication met with no better success than the *Meditations*, although Descartes had again written in Latin, and had been at pains to set out his teaching in a form that would make the work suitable for use as a college manual. Descartes ceased, henceforth, to hope for any sort of prompt official recognition. Instead he turned his attention once again to the common reader who had welcomed the *Discourse* and the *Essays*. The *Meditations* were soon put into French by the Duc de Luynes. Descartes then published a second edition of the *Meditations*, which included the objections he had solicited from various men of learning, together with his own replies, and he requested de Luynes to include them himself in a second edition of the French version of the work which Descartes had read, and on which he set the seal of his approval. Then, in 1647, came a French translation of the *Principles of Philosophy* together with an important Preface in the form of a letter to the anonymous translator, in which Descartes declares his general view of the function of philosophy and sums up his own achievement to date; and readers of this volume may be interested or amused to compare the studiously moderate and self-effacing language of the *Discourse* with the assured, almost aggressive, tone of the *Letter-Preface* with its strictures upon Aristotle in particular, and indeed upon all philosophy before Descartes' own.

For, by this time, despite the obduracy of the Sorbonne and the Jesuits, Descartes had become something of an international figure. He was renowned as the inventor of analytical geometry and of a new 'mathematical' method in the pursuit of knowledge of which the results were bound to be surprisingly fruitful, whatever the Sorbonne or the Jesuits might say. The roots of the tree of knowledge had been firmly planted in the *Meditations*, the trunk had grown, and the mechanical view of nature firmly established, for the laws of mechanics, he tells us in the *Letter-Preface*, are the laws of nature itself. We find him in these the last two or three years of his life cultivating the two remaining branches of knowledge: medicine and ethics; for a proper knowledge of medicine seemed to him, as he tells us in the *Discourse*, of all forms of knowledge the one most likely to be of benefit to the mental and moral, as well as the physical, progress of humanity, while the ethics with which he was now concerned was no longer the provisional ethics of the *Discourse*, but the ethics which, he says in the *Letter-Preface*, as it presupposes a knowledge of all the other sciences, is the crown and perfection of them all.

It was probably about this time too that Descartes wrote his unfinished dialogue, *The Search for Truth*, which begins with an elaborate account of the steps leading to the *cogito* and is more remarkable for showing the importance Descartes attached to his first truth than for literary grace. The dialogue form, which involves giving due importance to opinions which the author regards as irretrievably erroneous, was hardly suited to the forthright temperament of Descartes, and his main interest, during these last years, was undoubtedly in what he seems to have regarded as the twin sciences of medicine and ethics. However, it was in the latter, which arose from his correspondence with Elizabeth of Bohemia, that he made most progress. He had hoped that the study of medicine would at least teach him the means of prolonging life, but he was forced to admit failure. Thus in replying to a friend who had written to inquire what progress he had made in his researches, he observes: ' ... instead of finding the means of preserving my life, I have found another one, far

easier and safer, and that is how not to be afraid of death.'
And death, as it happens, was close at hand. By 1649, Descartes' work in ethics, the treatise on *The Passions of the Soul*,
was in the hands of the printers; but Descartes only lived
long enough to receive the first copies in Sweden, where he
had gone to instruct Queen Christina in the principles of his
philosophy, on her pressing invitation. The rigour of the
climate, and Christina's insistence upon receiving lessons from
her illustrious tutor in the early hours of the morning, however cold the weather, proved too much for his health which
had always required the greatest care. He caught cold, con-
tracted pleurisy, and died on 11 February 1650, some six
weeks before his fifty-fourth birthday.

6

Descartes is one of the great philosophers of the Western
world, and a great philosopher continues to live for posterity
less perhaps by the details of his doctrine than by the inspiration from which that doctrine grew, and by his influence upon
his successors, even those who prove to be his adversaries. To
read the *Discourse on Method* today is to receive an education in
the art of being a philosopher, whatever we may think of the
cogito; and the questions raised by Descartes lie at the roots of
modern philosophy. If we reject the *cogito*, or something like
it, where shall we begin, and where shall we end? In blind
faith for the one, and in scepticism, no doubt, for the other.
Nor will it be any consolation to accuse the sceptic, as
Bertrand Russell once suggested was the only recourse for
the philosopher, of insincerity. For Montaigne was not in-
sincere, and to lay one's head on the 'soft pillow' of scepticism
is not an impossible posture. Again, the problem of dualism,
however awkward it has proved, is a real problem, and indeed
it seems impossible not to accept some sort of dualism of
mind and matter, whatever subtleties we may employ to
disguise it. Then, Descartes' picture of the external world was
badly wrong in almost every detail; but the spirit which
inspired it is still largely that of modern physics. Finally, even
his ontological proof of the existence of God, however often
it may be controverted, still leaves a suspicion in the mind that

it may after all be valid. If we can conceive perfection as what we mean by God, can we mean anything by denying its real existence? The spirit, at least, of Cartesianism is still potent.

All this does not mean that we can accept the specific doctrine of Descartes as a whole; it does mean that the questions that exercised Descartes still affect us, and that it is as well to see how he answered them. Descartes himself would not have thanked us for this conclusion. He would have failed to see how the spirit of Cartesianism could be valuable if the Cartesian philosophy were in any way wrong. He was generous and modest, perfectly honest in his avowed contempt for worldly honours; he wished his philosophy to be of practical benefit to mankind; and he insisted that it was only his possession of an infallible method, which others could learn, which made him a philosopher. But he was not tolerant in the modern sense. He took ideas seriously, and so, while granting anyone the right to hold as true what he himself judged to be false, he could never have brought himself to think or to say that what he knew 'by the natural light of his mind' to be true, might after all be false. There was no room in his philosophy for mere opinion. He had undertaken to produce mathematically true demonstrations of all the propositions he put forward, and he was convinced that all knowledge was one, just as there was only one infallible method, so that where one science was right, all must be right, and where one science was wrong, all must be wrong. But a philosopher's philosophy is the hostage he gives to fortune; and fortune has decreed that Descartes was not to be, as he had hoped, the Aristotle of the modern world. Nevertheless, through his understanding of the philosophical predicament of his time, and through the influence his philosophy has exerted over his successors, he still deserves to be called, as he has been called by one of his modern adversaries, Jacques Maritain, the 'Great Innovator'.

*

The present translation includes the *Discourse on Method* and the *Meditations* which, despite their brevity, are the most important of the writings of Descartes. To these two works has been added the *Preface* to the *Principles of Philosophy*, in which Descartes put together his teachings in metaphysics and physics in the form of a college manual. The *Preface* was published in the form of a letter to the French translator of the *Principles*, which had originally appeared in Latin, and its considerable importance lies in the light it throws upon Descartes' own view of his work at a time when, despite the hostility of the Sorbonne, his name was becoming known all over Europe. For the convenience of the reader, each section of the *Discourse*, each *Meditation*, and the *Preface*, are preceded by a summary printed in italics.

A. J. W.

Discourse on Method

*

FOREWORD

*

IF this Discourse seems too long to be read at a sitting, one can divide it into six parts. In the first there are various considerations touching the sciences. The second contains the principal rules of the method the author has been seeking, and the third some of those rules of morality which he has derived from his method. The fourth part gives the reasons by which he proves the existence of God and of the human soul which are the foundation of his metaphysics. In the fifth part the author sets out the order of the problems in physics which he has examined, and makes particular reference to the explanation of the movement of the heart, to various other difficulties which belong to the science of medicine, and to the difference there is between the human and the animal soul. Finally, in the sixth part, the author explains what he thinks he requires in order to make further progress in his researches, and gives his reasons for writing.

[*The power of reasoning is naturally equal in all men. If this does not seem immediately evident, that is because all men do not know the right method of reasoning. But this method Descartes thinks he has had the good fortune to find, and his object in the* Discourse on Method *is to give a plain account of his discovery, its process and some of its results. The first step was to free himself from the education he had received. Estimable in itself, it had yet left him dissatisfied and in a state of uncertainty about almost everything. The course he followed was to leave aside his books and to turn instead to a study of the 'great book of the world' and of himself.*]

GOOD sense is of all things in the world the most evenly distributed amongst men, for each one thinks himself so well endowed with it that even those who are the most difficult to please in everything else are generally content with their share. And it seems incredible that all should be mistaken. Their common satisfaction points rather to the fact that the power of judging rightly, and of separating what is true from what is false (which is generally called good sense or reason), is equal by nature in all men. We differ in opinion, not because some of us have a larger share of reason than others, but because we think in different ways, and do not fix our attention upon the same objects. For it is not enough to have a good mind; the principal requirement is that we should apply it in the right way. The greatest souls are capable of the greatest vices, as well as of the greatest virtues; and those who move forward only very slowly may make far better progress, if only they keep to the right path, than those who rush on impetuously and go further and further astray.

For my part, I have never presumed to regard my mind as in any way more perfect than the average. Indeed, I have often wished my thoughts would move as rapidly and easily as is the case with some, that my imagination were as precise and clear, my memory as embracing and prompt, as theirs. Nor do I know of any other qualities than these that minister to the perfection of the mind. Reason itself, or good sense, inasmuch as it alone makes us men, and marks us off from the beasts, I must believe is found whole and entire in each man, following the opinion of those philosophers who affirm that, where individuals of the same species are concerned, there may be degrees in respect of their accidental qualities, but not in respect of their forms, or natures.

What I will say, however, without fear, is that my good fortune led me in early youth into a certain course of thought opening upon various considerations and principles, with the help of which I have formed a method designed, as I think, to provide me with what I require in order to increase my knowledge step by step, and to raise it gradually to the highest point to which the mediocrity of my talents, and the brief duration of my life, will allow it to attain. For the fruits of this method have already been so great that, although I endeavour always to distrust the conclusions I have reached by myself, rather than to presume upon them, and although, when I look with the eye of a philosopher upon the varied actions and projects of men, there is almost nothing that does not appear empty and unprofitable, I still harbour a feeling of the utmost satisfaction at the progress I think I have already made in the search for truth, and I still conceive such high hopes for the future that if, among the purely human occupations of men, there is one that may be regarded as of solid worth and importance, I dare believe that it is the one I have chosen.

Of course I may be mistaken, and what I take for gold and diamonds may be no more than a little brass, and some fragments of broken glass. I know how subject we are to error in what concerns us closely, and how suspicious we should be of the judgements delivered by our friends, when they pronounce in our favour. I should be glad, however, in this discourse, to describe for the benefit of others the paths I have followed, to paint a picture, as it were, of my life, of which each one may judge as he pleases; and I should be happy, too, to learn what public opinion has to say of me, and so discover a fresh mode of instruction for myself, which I shall add to those I am already accustomed to employ.

Thus, my present design is not to teach the method which each one is bound to employ for the proper conduct of his reason, but only to show how I have conducted mine. People who take it upon themselves to issue precepts must think themselves cleverer than those for whom they issue them; and, if they are found wanting in the least particular, they deserve reproof. But, since I offer what I have written simply as a record, or, if you prefer the term, a tale in which, with a few examples that may be followed, there will be many, perhaps, that it will be right to avoid, I hope that it will be useful to some, without being harmful to any, and that all will be grateful to me for my frankness.

Books formed my education from childhood, and, because I had been induced to believe that, with their help, I might acquire a clear and assured knowledge of everything that is of use in life, I felt an intense desire to learn from them. But, no sooner had I completed this whole course of study, at the end of which it is customary to take one's place in the ranks of the learned, then my opinion changed entirely. For I found myself hampered by so many doubts and errors that the only benefit of my efforts to become an educated person seemed to be the increasing discovery of my own ignorance. And yet I had been in one of the most famous schools in all Europe, in which, I thought, if anywhere in the world, there must be learned men. I had learned in it all that others learned.

Moreover, not content with what was taught me, I had perused all the books of occult and rarefied knowledge which had happened to fall into my hands. I knew the opinion others had of me, and it did not seem that I was regarded as inferior to my fellow-pupils, even though some of them were already destined to follow in the footsteps of our masters. The age in which we live seemed to me to be no less flourishing, no less fertile in good minds, than any of its predecessors. And so, in the end, I allowed myself the liberty of taking my own predicament as universal, and of concluding that nowhere in the world was there any knowledge professed of the kind I had been encouraged to expect.

For all that, my respect for the training we receive in school did not diminish. I knew that the languages we learn there are necessary for the understanding of ancient texts; that the tales those texts contain charm and waken the mind; that the memorable deeds they record exalt the mind, and, when considered with discernment, help to form the judgement; that the reading of good books is tantamount to a conversation with the most polished and eminent minds of the past, a sort of studied intercourse, indeed, in which the authors of these books reveal the best of their thoughts; that the eloquence of the orator is full of power, and contains unrivalled beauties of expression; that poetry ravishes with its subtle grace and sweetness; that mathematics has cunning inventions fit both to satisfy the curious mind, and to facilitate the exercise of the technician's skill; that moral treatises contain many instructions and many exhortations to virtue which are of the greatest use; that theology teaches us how to gain heaven; that philosophy enables us to speak plausibly of everything, and to win the admiration of the least learned, that jurisprudence, medicine, and the other branches of knowledge bring honours and riches to those who cultivate them; and, finally, that it is well to have examined them all, even those full of superstition and falsehood, so that we may take them at their proper value, and avoid becoming their dupes.

For my part, however, I thought that I had given enough time to the study of languages, and even to the reading of ancient texts, with their histories and their tales. For to live in the company of the men of other times is almost the same thing as to travel. It is good to know something about the manners and customs of other nations so that we may judge more sanely of our own, and may not think that whatever is contrary to our own mode of life is both ridiculous and unreasonable, as is usually the case with those who have seen nothing. But a man who has spent too much time in travelling becomes in the end a stranger in his own country; and a man who has too much curiosity about what happened in past centuries usually shows a great ignorance of what is happening in this one. These tales, moreover, make us imagine many events to be possible which are not so in fact; and even the most faithful record, although it may neither change the facts, nor enhance their value, in order to make them more worthy of being related, at least always omits the least dignified and the least illustrious circumstances. Thus, the rest does not appear such as it really was, and those who regulate their behaviour by the examples they derive from it are prone to fall into the extravagances that afflict the Paladins of our romances, and to conceive designs that exceed their powers.

I had a great esteem for eloquence, and I was in love with poetry; but I thought that both were gifts of the spirit rather than the fruits of study. Those who reason most cogently and who order their thoughts best, so as to make them clear and intelligible, are best able to persuade us of what they put forward, even when they speak in nothing but dialect and have learned nothing from the rhetorician; just as those whose imagination is the most pleasing, and who know best how to adorn and sweeten the expression of what they imagine, remain the best poets, even when they are completely ignorant of the *Art of Poetry*.[1]

Mathematics gave me most pleasure because of the certitude and evidential character of its reasonings; but I did not then perceive the true use to which mathematics can be put; and, as I considered that its only use was in the technical arts, I was struck with astonishment that a more imposing edifice had not been raised on such firm and solid foundations. As for the moral treatises of the ancients, I compared them, on the other hand, to proud and splendid palaces built upon sand and mud. They exalt the virtues to the skies, and make them seem more worthy of esteem than anything else in the world; but they do not teach us sufficiently how to recognize them, and often what they call by so fine a name is no more than lack of natural feeling, or a display of pride or despair, or an act of parricide. Our theology I revered, and was as eager as anyone else to gain heaven; but having learned, as a fully established fact, that the way thither is open to the most ignorant no less than to the most learned, and that the revealed truths, which guide us on our way, are above our understanding, I should not have dared to submit them to the weakness of my reasoning. Indeed, a man who undertook to investigate these truths and who succeeded in his task, would need, in my judgement, to be favoured with some special aid from heaven, and to be himself more than a man.

I shall say nothing of philosophy, save only this: in view of the fact that it has been cultivated by the most excellent minds that have appeared in this world for many centuries past, and that, nevertheless, every one of its propositions is still subject to dispute, and consequently to doubt, I had by no means enough presumption to hope

1. The reference is to the *Ars Poetica* of Horace.

that I should be more fortunate in it than the rest; and then, reflecting upon the number of different opinions that can be maintained by learned men on a single topic, although only one of these can ever be true, I came to regard as almost false whatever merely looked like the truth.

As for the other sciences whose principles are borrowed from philosophy, I judged that nothing stable could have been built on such insecure foundations; and neither the honour nor the wealth they promised were sufficiently inviting to persuade me to make a study of them. For, by the grace of God, my position in the world was not such as to oblige me to make a trade of knowledge in order to remedy my fortunes. I did not profess to despise glory, in the manner of a cynic, but I cared very little for the glory which I could acquire without a legitimate claim. Finally, I thought I knew enough about the false sciences not to run the risk any longer of being duped by the promises of the alchemist, the predictions of the astrologer, the impostures of the magician, by the tricks and bragging of any one of those who profess to know more than they do.

And so, for all these reasons, as soon as my age freed me from subjection to my tutors, I entirely abandoned the study of books. And, resolving henceforth to seek for no other knowledge than the knowledge I might find in myself, or else in the great book of the world, I spent the rest of my youth in travel, in visiting courts and armies, in seeking the company of men of varying character and rank, in gathering experience, in putting myself to the test in the encounters that came to me by chance, and in reflecting always and everywhere in such a way on the events with which I was confronted as to draw some benefit from my reflections. For it seemed to me that I should find more truth in the reasonings which a man makes with regard to matters which touch him closely, and of which the outcome must be to his detriment, if his judgement has been at fault, than in the reasonings of a man of learning in his study, whose speculations remain without effect, and are of no further consequence to him than that he may derive all the more vanity from them the further removed they are from good sense, because of the greater skill and ingenuity he has to employ to make them seem plausible. And I had, at all times, the utmost desire to learn how to distinguish between the true and the false so that I might see clearly into my own actions, and walk with assurance in this life.

It is true that so long as I did nothing but reflect upon the behaviour of other men, I found no grounds in it for assurance; indeed, I perceived in it as many divergences as I had found formerly in the opinions of the philosophers. Thus, the greatest benefit I derived from my observations was that, by noticing that many things which may seem to us quite extravagant and quite ridiculous are nevertheless commonly accepted with approval by other great nations, I learned not to believe too firmly in what only custom and example had persuaded me to accept as true; and, in this way, I freed myself, little by little, from many of those errors which obscure the natural light of the mind, and make us less capable of listening to reason. However, after I had spent some years in the study of the book of the world and in the effort to acquire experience, I resolved one day to study my own nature as well, and to employ all the resources of my mind to choose the paths which I ought to follow. And in this I succeeded much better, it seems to me, than I would have done had I never departed either from my country, or from my books.

2

[*Descartes describes the experience which came to him one day in a little village in Germany when, left to his own thoughts, alone in a stove-heated room, without any risk of interruption, he realized that his mind was so full of ill-founded opinions that he must sooner or later rid himself of them all. This was to envisage a reform of the human mind, and such a task could only be undertaken by a single person. But Descartes did not entertain the foolish ambitions of a professed reformer. His reform was a personal matter, the reform of his own mind, and his example might well be a dangerous one for most men to follow. There were, however, certain rules – four, to be exact – which must be strictly followed in the search for truth, and we learn best how to apply them in the solution of mathematical or quasi-mathematical problems. Thus would the foundation be laid of certainty in all the forms of knowledge. For the moment, however, Descartes felt himself too young and inexperienced to embark upon the immense task of laying this foundation, and so he spent the next nine years in gathering experience and in the assiduous practice of his method.]*

I WAS at one time in Germany, attracted thither by the wars which are not yet ended, and was on my way from the coronation of the Emperor to join the army, when winter brought me to a halt in quarters where, with no society to distract me, and no cares or passions to disturb me, I spent the day in a stove-heated room, with all the leisure in the world to occupy myself with my own thoughts. Among these, one of the first that came to my mind was that there is often less perfection in what has been put together bit by bit, and by different masters, than in the work of a single hand. Thus we see how a building, the construction of which has been undertaken and completed by a single architect, is usually superior in beauty and regularity to those that many have tried to restore by making use of old walls which had been built for other purposes. So, too, those old places which, beginning as villages, have developed in the course of time into great towns, are generally so ill-proportioned in comparison with those an engineer can design[1] at will

1. Descartes is thinking of the new fortified towns of Nancy (1588) and Charleville (1605).

in an orderly fashion that, even though the buildings taken severally often display as much art as in other places, or even more, yet the disorder is such with a large house here and a small one there, and the streets all tortuous and uneven, that the whole place seems to be the product of chance rather than the design of men who use their reason. And, if we reflect that nevertheless there have been at all times officials charged with the task of keeping watch over private building and making it serve the public interest, we will easily understand how difficult it is to achieve any degree of perfection by adding to the work of others. In the same way I fancied that half-savage nations, who had gradually become civilized, but who had made their laws by degrees as the need arose to counter the harm done by crimes and disputes, could never be as well regulated as those who, from the beginning of their associations, had observed the decrees of some prudent lawgiver; just as the religion for which the ordinances come from God alone must be incomparably better ordered than any other. Or, to take a purely human instance, I believe that Sparta flourished so well, not because of the excellence of its laws taken one by one, for some were extremely strange and even morally repugnant, but because, being all the invention of one man, they all tended towards the same end. Then what we learn from books, from those, at least, that contain only probabilities and no demonstrative arguments, and which are swollen with the opinions of a variety of authors, is further from the truth than the simple reasonings of a man of good sense with regard to what he observes or encounters. Finally, I reflected that, as we have all been children before becoming men, long governed by our appetites and our tutors, the former being often thwarted by the latter, and neither, perhaps, always giving the best counsel, it is almost impossible that our judgements should be as clear and as well-founded as they would have been if we had had the use of our reason from birth and had never been governed by anything else.

We do not, it is true, see people pulling down the houses of a whole town simply for the purpose of rebuilding them and rendering the streets more beautiful. But we do see many individuals engaged in this task of demolition and reconstruction, being sometimes constrained to do so because the houses are in danger of falling down and the foundations are insecure. With this as my example, I am convinced that, while on the one hand it would be truly absurd for an individual to undertake a reform of the State, by changing its foundations, and by overturning it in order to raise it up again, or to undertake a reform of the body of the sciences, or even of the established order of instruction in our schools, on the other hand, I could not do better than to undertake to rid myself, at least once in my life, of all the opinions I had hitherto accepted on faith, in order either to replace them with better ones or to restore them to their former place, once I had brought them to the level of my reason. And I firmly believed that, in this way, I should succeed in ordering my life much better than if I simply built upon the old foundations, and based myself upon principles I had allowed myself to adopt in youth, without ever considering whether they were true. For, although I see the difficulties of such a course, these difficulties are not without remedy, nor are they comparable with the reform of the least thing concerning the State. These great bodies are too awkward to raise up again, once they have been brought down, or even to hold up once they have been shaken, and their fall is bound to be rough and heavy. Then, as to their imperfections, if they have any (and the diversity among the forms of State assures us that they have), these are doubtless softened by use, which may even imperceptibly avert or correct a number of them which are not so easily remedied by foresight. Finally, these deficiencies are almost always more tolerable than a change; it is in this case as with those highroads winding along the mountainside which have become so smooth and convenient through constant use that it is far better to follow them than to attempt a straighter way by scaling rocks and clambering down precipices.

That is why I could in no way approve those cloudy and unquiet spirits who, being called neither by birth nor fortune to the handling of public affairs, are forever reforming the State in imagination; and, if I thought that there was the least thing in what I have written to bring me under suspicion of such folly, I should deeply regret its publication. My design has never stretched further than the attempted reform of my own thoughts and a reconstruction on foundations that belong only to me. If, since what I have done has pleased me well enough, I display it as a model, that does not mean that I advise anyone to follow it. Those to whom God has been more prodigal of His gifts will have designs of a higher order; I am only afraid that mine will prove too bold for many. The mere resolution to rid oneself of all one's former beliefs is not an example to be followed by everyone; and the world is almost made up of two types of minds to whom it is highly unsuitable. There are those who, thinking themselves cleverer than they are, have no power to stay the precipitancy of their judgements, and lack the patience to conduct their thoughts in due order, with the result that, having once taken the liberty of doubting accepted principles, and of straying from the common path, they would never be able to keep to the road that leads straight forward, and would remain wanderers all their lives. Then there are those who have enough good sense or modesty to know that they are less capable of distinguishing between the true and the false than some by whom they can be instructed, and who should be content to follow the opinions of others rather than seek out better ones for themselves.

As for myself, I should be counted among these last, had I ever had only one instructor, and had I not been aware of the divergencies of opinion that have always existed among the most learned. But, from my school-days, I had known that nothing so strange and so little credible can be imagined but some philosopher has been found to assert it. Later on I found, during my travels, that those who entertain notions that contradict our own are not, for that reason, barbarians or savages, but that many of them use their reason as much as we do, or even more. Finally, I considered how different a man of the same disposition would be if he had been brought up from childhood among Frenchmen or Germans, or if he had lived all his life with Chinese or cannibals, and how our very fashions in dress change, so that what pleased us ten years ago and will please us again ten years hence, now seems extravagant and worthy of ridicule. I observed, in fact, that what makes our convictions is custom and example rather than any sort of assured knowledge, while, on the other hand, a plurality of votes is of no avail in the discovery of difficult truths, since it is much more likely that they would be found by a single person than by a whole people. Thus I could choose no one whose opinions I might prefer to those of others, and I was as if condemned to be my own guide through life.

I determined, however, like a man who walks alone in the darkness, to go forward so slowly, and with so much circumspection at every step, that, even if I made very little progress, I should at least avoid a fall. I was even unwilling to cast aside all those beliefs which might have slipped into my mind without the agency of my reason before I had spent enough time in planning the work I was undertaking, and in seeking out the true method of attaining to the knowledge of all that was within the capacity of my mind.

In my early youth, I had made some study of logic in philosophy, and of geometry and algebra in mathematics, and it seemed that these three arts or sciences should contribute something to my design. But, when I examined them more closely, I saw that, as for logic, its syllogisms and most of its other modes of instruction rather serve to explain to others what one knows already, or even, as in the art of Lully,[1] to speak without judgement of what one does not know, than to acquire knowledge. And, although logic indeed contains many very true and excellent precepts, these are so confounded with so many others that are either harmful or superfluous that it is as difficult to distinguish the former as it would be to conjure up a statue of Diana or Minerva from an untouched block of marble. Then, with regard to the geometrical analysis of the ancients and the algebra of the moderns, besides the fact that both only deal with what is highly abstract and seems of no practical use, the former is so bound to the inspection of figures that it cannot exercise the understanding without greatly fatiguing the imagination, while the other is so subject to certain rules and a certain notation that it has become a confused and obscure art, which clogs the mind, rather than a science which cultivates its powers. That is why I thought I must look for some other method which would combine the advantages of these three disciplines, and yet be exempt from their defects. And, as a multiplicity of laws often provides excuses for vice, so that a State is much better governed when its few laws are very strictly observed, so, in place of the many precepts of which logic is composed, I thought I should have enough with the four following rules, provided I took a firm and constant resolution never once to fail to observe them.

1. The *Ars Magna* of Raymond Lully (1235–1315).

The first rule was to accept as true nothing that I did not know to be evidently so: that is to say, to avoid carefully precipitancy and prejudice, and to apply my judgements to nothing but that which showed itself so clearly and distinctly to my mind that I should never have occasion to doubt it.

The second was to divide each difficulty I should examine into as many parts as possible, and as would be required the better to solve it.

The third was to conduct my thoughts in an orderly fashion, starting with what was simplest and easiest to know, and rising little by little to the knowledge of the most complex, even supposing an order where there is no natural precedence among the objects of knowledge.

The last rule was to make so complete an enumeration of the links in an argument, and to pass them all so thoroughly under review, that I could be sure I had missed nothing.

Those long chains of reasons, all quite simple and quite easy, which geometers are wont to employ in reaching their most difficult demonstrations, had given me occasion to imagine that all the possible objects of human knowledge were linked together in the same way, and that, if we accepted none as true that was not so in fact, and kept to the right order in deducing one from the other, there was nothing so remote that it could not be reached, nothing so hidden that it could not be discovered. And I was little troubled to know where to begin; for I already knew that it was by what was simplest and easiest to know; and, reflecting that among all those who have sought after truth in the sciences only the mathematicians have been able to adduce a few proofs, that is to say, certain and evident reasons, I did not doubt that I should begin with what they had investigated, although for no other benefit than to accustom my mind to nourish itself on truth. It was no part of my design, however, to attempt to learn all those particular sciences which go under the general name of mathematics. Seeing that, although they have different objects, they yet agree in all being concerned with nothing but the relations or proportions between terms, I thought it best simply to consider these proportions in general, without considering their existence except in the objects which gave me knowledge of them, and without even restricting them to these objects so as to be the better able to apply them wherever they should fit. Then, as I became aware that, in order to know them, I should sometimes have to consider each one in particular, and sometimes only keep them in my memory, or take several together, I thought that, the better to consider each separately, I should represent them as straight lines, which was the simplest way I could think of and the most easily grasped by my imagination and my senses, but that, in order to retain them in my memory, or to take several together, I should explain them by certain symbols which should be as concise as possible. And in this way I thought I should be able to borrow the best there is in both geometrical analysis and algebra, and to correct the defects of the one by the other.[1]

Indeed, I venture to say that the exact observance of the few rules I had chosen made it so easy for me to disentangle all the problems raised by these two sciences that, within the two or three months I spent in examining them, I was able, by beginning with what was simplest and most general, and by using each discovery as a means of finding fresh truths, not only to overcome much that I had judged to be extremely difficult, but it seemed to me that, even in matters of which I was ignorant, I could determine in what way, and to what extent, a solution might be found. Nor will this seem vanity on my part, if you consider that, as there is only one truth about

1. Descartes is referring to his discovery of analytical geometry.

anything, he who discovers it knows as much about the matter as can be known; thus a child who has been taught arithmetic and has done an addition according to the rules, has found out as much about the total he has been considering as the human mind can find. For, after all, the method which teaches us to follow the right order, and to enumerate exactly all the elements of a problem, covers everything that gives certainty to the rules of arithmetic.

But what pleased me most, however, about this method, was that by means of it I was sure of always using my reason, if not perfectly, at least as well as lay within my power. Besides, I felt that the practice of this method was accustoming my mind to conceiving the objects of knowledge with greater clarity and distinction, and, as it was subjected to no particular branch of learning, I promised myself that I would apply it as effectively to the difficulties of the other sciences as I had done to those of algebra. Not that I dared to undertake to investigate all these sciences from the start as they presented themselves; for that would have been contradictory to the order prescribed by my method. I had observed that the principles of these sciences must be taken from philosophy, in which, however, I found no assured principles, and I thought that my first task must be to establish such principles. But this is the most important task in the world, and the one in which haste and prejudice are most to be feared, and I felt I should not undertake it until I had reached a more mature age than the age of twenty-three, as I was at that time, and until I had spent a good deal of time in preparing myself for it, both by uprooting all the wrong notions that had hitherto inhabited my mind, and by accumulating observations to form the matter of my reasonings, and, finally, by constantly exercising myself in my prescribed method so as to strengthen myself more and more in its use.

[*But a man who undertakes to strip his mind of all his previous notions must still have certain principles to live by; the everyday business of living cannot be adjourned. Descartes declares his adherence to the Catholic religion in which he has been brought up, and gives a sketch of a provisional morality based largely upon the Stoic tradition, with moderation as the regulating virtue.*]

Now it is not enough, before beginning to rebuild the house in which one lives, simply to pull it down, to provide for building materials and architects, or to become one's own architect, and, besides all this, to have a careful plan drawn up for the new construction, but one must have some other convenient place in which to reside while the work of building goes on; and, in the same way, in order that I might not remain irresolute in my actions while reason obliged me to suspend my judgement, but might continue to live as happily as I could, I devised a provisional morality for myself, composed of only three or four maxims, which I am willing to disclose.

The first was to obey the laws and customs of my country, adhering to the religion in which God had given me the grace to be instructed since childhood, and governing myself in everything in accordance with the most moderate opinions, that is to say, those least given to excess, as commonly accepted in practice by the most sensible of those among whom I should have to live. For, as I had already begun to count my own opinions as nothing, being resolved to review them all, I was sure I could not do better than follow those of the most sensible. There may, it is true, be people just as sensible among the Persians and the Chinese as among us, but I thought it more expedient to regulate my behaviour according to those with whom I should have to live. And I also thought that, in order to know their real sentiments, I should observe their actions rather than their words, not only because the corruption of our manners and customs makes most people unwilling to declare what they believe, but because many do not know it themselves; for the activity of thought by which we believe something is different from the activity by which we know we believe, so that the one can exist without the other. Again, among several generally approved opinions, I always chose the more moderate ones, as being the easier to put into practice and the more likely to be the better ones, since all excess is usually bad; besides, I should be straying less far from the right path, if the opinion were wrong, than if, of two extremes, I chose the wrong one. In particular, I included among the forms of excess all those promises by which we deprive ourselves of some of our freedom. Not that I disapprove of those laws which attempt to remedy the inconstancy of weaker spirits by allowing for the making of vows in the case of some pious design, and of contracts to safeguard commerce in the case of some secular plan, both of which enforce perseverance. As, however, I saw nothing in the world that always remained the same, and as, in my case particularly, I was promising myself constantly to improve my powers of judgement, and not to make them worse, I should have regarded it as a crime against good sense to oblige myself, because I had once approved of something, to approve of it again at some later time, when either it was no longer good, or I had ceased to regard it as such.

My second maxim was to be as firm and resolute in my actions as I could, and to adhere as strongly to the most dubious opinion, once I had resolved upon it, as if it were the most assured, thus imitating travellers lost in a forest who should not wander about, turning now this way, now that, still less stand still in one place, but should move straight forward, as well as they can, in the same direction, without allowing some slight reason to induce them to deflect their steps, even though it was chance alone that first made them choose a way; for, in this manner, even if they do not reach their destination, they will at least get somewhere in the end where they will no doubt be better off than in the middle of a forest. Now, as the actions of life often suffer no delay, it is very certainly true that, when it is not in our power to distinguish the truest opinions, we must choose the most probable ones; and, furthermore, when we do not observe any degrees of probability as between various opinions, we must, nevertheless, resolve upon some among them and consider them thenceforth, in respect of our actions, as quite true and quite certain, our reason for thus resolving ourselves being in itself quite true and quite certain. Thus was I immediately delivered from those fits of repentance and remorse which commonly agitate weak and ill-balanced spirits who allow themselves, inconsequently, to practise as good what they afterwards judge to be bad.

My third maxim was always to attempt the mastery over myself rather than over fortune, to try to alter my desires rather than the course of the world, and in general to accustom myself to the belief that there is nothing that lies wholly within our power save our thoughts, so that once we have done our best in respect of what is external to us, we may regard what we fail to achieve as absolutely impossible. And this consideration is enough by itself, as it seems to me, to make me desire nothing I do not get, and so to make me content. For, as our will naturally only tends to desire those things which the understanding represents as possible to it, it is certain that, if we look upon all external goods as equally outside our power, we should no more regret the loss of what seems due to our birth, if we have been deprived of it through no fault of our own, than we regret not being in possession of the realms of China and Mexico. In the same way, making a virtue of necessity, as the saying goes, we should no more desire to be well, when we are ill, or to be free, when we are in prison, than we now wish we had bodies as incorruptible as diamonds, or long for wings with which to fly like birds. I admit, however, that long practice and repeated meditation are required to accustom oneself to seeing things in this way, and, I believe that their power to do so was the principal secret of those philosophers[1] who were able, in ancient times, to withdraw themselves from the empire of chance, and, despite sorrows and poverty, to claim to be as happy as the gods. Constantly occupied in considering the limitations imposed upon them by nature, they were so perfectly convinced that nothing lay within their power except their thoughts that this was enough to prevent them from any leaning towards anything else; while of these thoughts they disposed so absolutely that they had thereby some reason for regarding themselves as richer, more powerful, freer, and happier than any other man who, without this philosophy, and however much he might be favoured by nature and fortune, could never have the same mastery over anything he wanted.

Finally, as a conclusion to this moral code of mine, I thought of reviewing carefully the various occupations of men in this life with the object of choosing the best among them, and, without wishing to say anything about other avocations, I thought I could not do better than persevere in my own, employing all my days in cultivating my reason, and in advancing, as well as I could, in the knowledge of the truth according to the method I had prescribed for myself. For I had experienced such extreme contentment since I had begun to make use of this method, that I did not think I could feel any sweeter or more innocent pleasure in this life. Each day I discovered, with the help of my method, truths that seemed

1. The Stoics.

important enough, and which were commonly unknown to others, and my satisfaction so filled my mind that nothing else affected it. Besides, the three preceding maxims were all based on nothing but the plan I had made of continuing to instruct myself. For, as God has given each one of us some power of distinguishing between the true and the false, I should not have thought that I ought to content myself with the opinions of others for a single moment, had I not made up my mind to exercise my judgement on them at the proper time; nor should I have been able to free myself of every scruple in following them, if I had not hoped to lose no opportunity thereby of finding better ones, in case there were any. Finally, I should not have known how to limit my desires, nor how to be happy, if I had not followed a path which would, as I thought, not only lead me to the acquisition of all the knowledge of which I should ever be capable, but also, and in the same manner, of all the real wealth which would ever lie within my reach. For, as the will never brings itself to pursue or to avoid anything except as the understanding represents it as good or bad, it is enough to judge well to do well, and to judge as well as one can in order to do one's best, in order to acquire, that is to say, all the virtues, as well as all the other goods together that we are capable of acquiring. And when one is certain that all this is true, one cannot fail to be happy.

Once I had made certain of the truth of these maxims, and had set them aside, together with the truths of faith which have always ranked first in my belief, I judged that I might freely rid myself of the rest of my opinions. And, as I hoped to be able to deal with them better through the society of other men than by remaining any longer shut up in the stove-heated room in which these thoughts had come to me, winter had hardly come to an end before I set out upon my travels again.

For the next nine years, then, I did nothing but wander from place to place in the world, endeavouring to appear as a spectator rather than to act a part in any of its comedies; and, by taking particular heed of what seemed dubious and where misapprehension might arise, I up-rooted meanwhile from my mind all the errors that had previously crept in. Not that I was imitating those sceptics who doubt for the sake of doubting, and effect to be always undecided; on the contrary, my whole object was always to achieve certainty, and to probe beneath the shifting soil and the sands to find the underlying rock or stone. Nor were my efforts unrewarded, as it seems to me, for in seeking to discover the falseness or the un-certainty of the propositions I examined, not by feeble conjectures, but by clear and assured reasonings, I found none so dubious that I was unable to draw a sufficiently certain conclusion from it, even if this conclusion was simply that there was nothing certain about it. Again, just as when an old dwelling is pulled down the demolished parts are set aside for the new building, so, in destroying all those of my opinions which I judged to be ill-founded, I made various observations, and acquired many experi-ences which have since been of use to me in establishing other, more certain, notions. Furthermore, I continued in the exercise of my prescribed method, and besides taking care to conduct my thoughts in general according to its rules, I reserved a few hours, now and again, specially for the solution of mathematical difficulties, and even of those I could assimilate to mathematical ones, by detaching them from the principles which I had not found sufficiently well-established of the other sciences, as you will see I have done in the case of many problems I have dealt with further on in this volume.[1] And so, while appearing to live like those who, having no other employ-

1. The *Discourse on Method* was originally published as a preface to three essays. See Introduction.

ment than to spend gentle and innocent lives, take pains to distinguish between pleasure and vice, and who, in order to enjoy their leisure without tedium, indulge in every honest diversion, I continued to persevere in my design, and to advance further in the knowledge of the truth, more perhaps than if I had done nothing but read books and cultivate the society of men of letters.

However, those nine years went by before I had taken up a position with regard to the difficulties which are commonly debated by the learned, or had begun to look for the foundations of a philosophy more certain than the common one. And the example afforded me by certain eminent thinkers who had previously conceived such a design, but had fallen short of success, made me imagine great difficulty in this enterprise, and I should not have dared to attempt it so soon were it not that there were rumours going about that I had already brought it to a successful conclusion. I cannot tell on what these rumours were based; and, if I have contributed anything to them by my words, it must have been by confessing my ignorance of certain things more ingenuously than is the habit with those who have acquired some learning, and perhaps also by displaying the reasons I had for doubting many things which others regarded as certain, rather than by boasting of my knowledge in any direction. Nevertheless, I had enough pride not to wish to be taken for other than I was, and thought I should endeavour, in every way, to make myself worthy of my reputation. Eight years ago exactly, with this in mind, I resolved to live far from the places in which I had acquaintances, and to retire to this country[1] in which a long war has established such discipline that the sole object of the army it maintains seems to be to safeguard the benefits of peace. Here, amid a multitude of busy people, more concerned with their

1. Descartes retired to Holland in 1629. The *Discourse on Method* was published eight years later in 1637.

own business than curious about the affairs of others, without missing any of the conveniences that are found in thickly populated cities, I have been able to live as solitary and undisturbed as in the most remote of deserts.

4

[*In this section of the* Discourse, *Descartes gives a summary of his metaphysical doctrine. His object is to show that his method leads to a twofold metaphysical certainty: the certainty of his own existence, and the certainty of the existence of God. The first gives a criterion of truth: whatever I perceive clearly and distinctly, by the natural light of the mind, I can take as true; and, in the same way, I know what I am – a thinking substance, quite distinct from the body which is an extended substance. The second certainty makes God, who is Perfection, the guarantor of all our knowledge; and, thus doubly armed, we can dispel all the doubts we have hitherto entertained.*]

I DO not know whether I should include in my discourse the first meditations that occupied my solitude; they are so metaphysical, and so much out of the ordinary, that they may not be to everybody's taste. And yet, to allow people to judge whether my starting-point is sufficiently secure, I feel obliged, in a sense, to speak of them. I had noticed long ago, as I have already pointed out, that, in matters of morality and custom, it is often necessary to follow opinions one knows to be highly doubtful, just as if there were no doubts attaching to them at all. Now, however, that I intended to make the search for truth my only business, I thought it necessary to do exactly the opposite, and to reject as absolutely false anything which gave rise in my mind to the slightest doubt, with the object of finding out, once this had been done, whether anything remained which I could take as indubitable. And so, because our senses sometimes deceive us, I made up my mind to suppose that they always did. Then, since there are men who fall into logical errors when they reason, even in the simplest geometrical matters, I reflected that I was as fallible as anyone, and rejected as false all the arguments I had hitherto regarded as conclusive. Finally, in view of the fact that those very same ideas, which come to us when we are awake, can also come when we are asleep without one of them then being true, I resolved to pretend that everything that had ever entered my mind was as false as the figments of my dreams. But then, immediately, as I strove to think of everything as false, I realized that, in the very act of thinking everything false, I was aware of myself as something real; and observing that the truth: *I think, therefore I am,* was so firm and so assured that the most extravagant arguments of the sceptics were incapable of shaking it, I concluded that I might have no scruple in taking it as that first principle of philosophy for which I was looking.

My next step was to examine attentively what I was, and here I saw that, although I could pretend that I had no body, and that there was neither world nor place in which I existed, I could by no means pretend that I myself was non-existent; on the contrary, from the mere fact that I could think of doubting the truth of other things, it followed quite clearly and evidently that I existed; whereas I should have had no reason to believe in my existence, had I but ceased to think for a moment, even if everything I had ever imagined had been true. I concluded that I was a substance whose whole essence or nature consists in thinking, and whose existence depends neither on its location in space nor on any material thing. Thus the self, or rather the soul, by which I am what I am, is entirely distinct from the body, is indeed easier to know than the body, and would not cease to be what it is, even if there were no body.

Next, I turned to a general consideration of what is required to ensure the truth and certitude of a proposition. I had just discovered one proposition of which I knew the truth to be assured, and I thought I should be able to learn in what this certitude consists. Observing that there is nothing in the proposition: *I think, therefore I am*, to assure me that I am speaking the truth, except that I see very clearly and distinctly that, in order to exist, one must think, I concluded that I could take as a general rule that the things we conceive very clearly and distinctly are all of them true, but that there is some difficulty in the proper discernment of distinct propositions.

Then, from reflecting on the fact that I had doubts, and that consequently my existence was not wholly perfect (for I saw clearly that it was a greater perfection to know than to doubt), it occurred to me to enquire how I had learned to think of something more perfect than myself, and it became evident to me that it must be through some nature which was in fact more perfect. As for the notions I had of many other things outside my mind, such as the sky, the earth, light, heat, and a thousand other things, I was not so much concerned to know whence these notions came to me, for I could see nothing in them that seemed to make them superior to me; if they were true, they came within the compass of my mind, insofar as my nature had any perfection,[1] and if false, they arose out of nothing, inhabiting my mind only through some imperfection in my nature. But this could not be the case with the idea of a being more perfect than myself, for it was manifestly impossible that this idea should come to me from nothing; and I could not have acquired it of myself, since it is as repugnant to reason that the more perfect should proceed from the less perfect, and be dependent upon it, as it is that something should come out of nothing. I could only conclude that it had been placed in my mind by a nature really more perfect than mine, possessing indeed every perfection of which I could have

1. See Note on Cartesian Terminology, p. 191.

any idea; that is to say, to express my meaning in a word, it had been placed in my mind by God. And I reflected further that I was not the only being that existed, for I knew that I lacked certain perfections, and that there must be, of necessity, some being more perfect than myself, on which I depended for my existence, and through which I had acquired every quality I possessed. For, if I had existed alone, in absolute independence of any other being, and possessing of myself the few qualities in which I participated through the perfect being, I might have had of myself, for the same reason, all those additional perfections I knew to be lacking in me. I could have been infinite, eternal, unmoved, all-knowing, and all powerful; I could have had all the perfections which I could see as existing in God. For, according to my reasoning so far, in order to know the nature of God insofar as my nature was capable of doing so, I had only to consider, with regard to each characteristic of which I had any idea, whether it were a measure of perfection, or not, to possess it; for I was sure that none of those that revealed any trace of imperfection was to be found in God, but that all the rest were. Thus I saw that doubt, inconsistency, melancholy, and so forth, were excluded from His nature, for I should have been glad to be exempt from them myself. There was also the fact that I had in my mind the ideas of many sensible and corporeal objects; I could suppose that I was dreaming, and that nothing I saw or imagined corresponded with the external reality, but I still could not deny that those ideas were really in my mind. But I had already seen clearly, by an examination of myself, that the intellectual nature is distinct from the corporeal, and so, considering that that which is composed of parts bears witness thereby to its contingent character, and that to be contingent is obviously an imperfection, I concluded that it could not be a mark of perfection in God to be composed of these two natures, and that consequently He was not so composed; and I also concluded that, if there were any bodies in the world, or any pure intelligences or any other beings which were not wholly perfect, their existence must depend on His power, in such a way that, without Him, they could not exist for a single moment.

Next, I sought to discover other truths, and, turning to the object studied by geometers, I conceived it to be a continuous body, or space indefinitely extended in length, breadth, and depth, and divisible into a variety of parts, which could assume different figures and sizes, and which could be moved and transposed in all sorts of ways; for all this is what geometers suppose in the object of their study, and so I went through some of their simplest proofs. I took note that the great certainty everyone attributes to these demonstrations is based upon the fact that they can be evidently understood, in accordance with the rule I have stated above, but I also observed that there was nothing in these demonstrations to assure me of the existence of their objects. For I saw clearly that, if I supposed a triangle, its three angles must be equal to two right angles, but I saw nothing, for all that, to make me sure that any triangle existed anywhere in the world. On the contrary, when I turned back to reconsider the idea I had of a perfect being,[1] I found that existence was included in it, just as the property of having its three angles equal to two right angles is included in the idea of a triangle, or the property of having its sides equidistant from its centre is included in the idea of a sphere; indeed, my first contention is the most evident of the three. It follows that it is as certain as any geometrical proof can be that God, who is this perfect being, is or exists.

What persuades people that it is difficult to know God, or even to know what their own souls are, is that they

1. See Note on Cartesian Terminology, p. 191.

never raise their minds above the objects of their senses, and are so accustomed to think of nothing without the help of their imaginations, that anything they cannot imagine seems to them unintelligible. This is clearly shown by the fact that it is a maxim among philosophers that there can be nothing in the understanding that has not first been in the senses, although it is certain that the ideas of God and of the soul have never been in the senses. It seems to me that those who wish to use their imaginations in order to understand God and the soul are like those who, in order to hear a sound, or to smell an odour, wish to make use of their eyes, with this difference, however, that the sense of sight assures us of the practical truth of its object, just as the senses of hearing and smell do, whereas neither the imagination nor the senses can give us certainty about anything without the intervention of the understanding.

Finally, if there are still some people who are not sufficiently convinced of the existence of God and of the soul, let me assure them that everything else of which they perhaps feel sure, as that they have bodies, that there are stars and the earth, and so on, is less certain. Of course, we have a moral certainty of these things which makes it seem impossible to doubt them without extravagance; but when it is a case of metaphysical certainty, we have enough cause for not being entirely sure, if we note that we can, in the same way, imagine ourselves in sleep to be possessed of another body, and to be seeing another earth and other stars. How do we know that the notions that come to us in dreams are false rather than the others, since they are often no less vivid and distinct? Let the best minds study the matter as long as they please, I do not believe they will find a reason good enough to remove this doubt, without presupposing the existence of God.

In the first place, the very rule I have already stated,

namely, that everything we conceive very clearly and distinctly is true, is only assured by the fact that God exists, that He is the perfect being, and that whatever we possess comes from Him. It follows that our ideas or notions, as they are real, and as they come from Him, insofar as they are clear and distinct, cannot but be true. If we often have ideas that contain untruths, these can only be those that are confused and obscure because they participate in nothingness, that is to say that we have them in this confused state because we are not perfect beings. It is evident that it would be as repugnant to the reason for falseness and imperfection to come from God, as such, as for truth and perfection to proceed from nothing. But if we did not know that everything we have that is real and true comes to us from a perfect and infinite being, however clear and distinct our ideas might be, we should have no reason to be sure that they had the perfection of truth.

Now, once the knowledge of God and of the soul has made us certain of the criterion of truth, it is easy to understand that what we dream, when we are asleep, should in no way make us doubt the truth of our thoughts when we are awake. For, if one happened to have a very distinct idea when one was asleep, if, for example, a geometer should invent a new proof in his sleep, his sleep would not prevent it from being true. As for the commonest error of our dreams, when they represent objects to us in the same way as our external senses do, it does not matter that it should make us suspicious of the truth of such ideas, for our senses also deceive us often enough without our being asleep. Thus a man with jaundice sees everything yellow, and the stars and other very distant bodies seem much smaller than they are. The fact is, whether we are asleep or awake, we should never be convinced of anything but by the evidence accepted by our reason.

It is to be observed that I speak of the reason, and not of the senses or the imagination. We see the sun very clearly, but it is not, for that reason, to be judged to be of the size we observe; and, although we can distinctly imagine the head of a lion grafted on to the body of a goat, that is no reason for concluding that any such monster exists in the world. Reason does not dictate to us that what we see or imagine is real, but it does dictate to us that all our ideas and notions must have some foundation of truth, for it would not be possible for God, who is Perfection and Truth, to put them in our minds, if this were not so. And so, as our reasonings are never so evident or so complete in sleep as when we are awake, although our imaginings are sometimes more vivid and more distinct in the former case, reason also dictates to us that, although our thoughts cannot always be true since we are not all-perfect, the truth is to be found certainly in our waking thoughts rather than in our dreams.

5

[*Descartes turns from metaphysics to physics. He gives a summary account of what he had written on the subject in the treatise he had laid aside at the moment of the condemnation of Galileo. Let us imagine a state of mere chaos, then a world would emerge exactly similar to ours, provided only God had implanted in it the laws of nature as we discern them and continued throughout time to sustain its existence. We may take the heart as an example of Descartes' physical conceptions. Harvey's theory is in many ways correct, but the heart is a machine set in motion by a certain warmth generated in it. In fact the human body is itself a machine, regulated by the animal spirits. And animals too are machines; if they were not, they would talk, and therefore reason, like men. But the human soul or mind is wholly distinct from the body, and we may plausibly infer that it does not die with the body, but is immortal.*]

I SHOULD be very glad to go on and display the whole chain of truths that I have deduced from these first ones;

but, as I should then have to introduce a number of questions which are still a matter of controversy among the learned, and as I do not wish to be at odds with any of them, I think it would be better to abstain from doing so, mentioning them only in a general way, and leaving it to the wisest to decide whether it would be to the advantage of the public to be more fully informed. It has always been my firm resolution never to suppose any other principle than the one I have just used in proving the existence of God and of the soul, and never to accept as true anything that did not seem to me even clearer and more certain than the geometrical proofs I had previously examined. Nevertheless, I dare affirm that I have not only been able to satisfy myself, within a short time, regarding the common problems of philosophy, but I have also discerned certain laws which have been so firmly established in nature by God, and of which the notions have been so firmly implanted in our minds by Him, that, with sufficient reflection, we cannot doubt their being strictly observed in everything that is, or that happens, in the world. Then, by observing the sequence of these laws, I seemed to have discovered many truths of greater use and greater importance than anything I had previously learned, or had even hoped to learn.

Now, as I have attempted to expound the chief among these truths in a treatise,[1] which certain considerations prevent me from publishing, I could not make them better known than by indicating summarily what this treatise contains. My intention was to include all that I thought I had learned, before I began to write, regarding the nature of material things. Now a painter, who is unable to represent on his flat canvas all the sides of a solid body, chooses one of the principal ones, setting it fully in the

1. The treatise is the 'World' which Descartes laid aside when it was on the verge of publication after the condemnation of Galileo. See Introduction, p. 17.

light and leaving the others in shadow so that we see them only in relation to the point of focus, and so, as I was afraid I should be unable to put into my discourse all that was in my mind, I undertook merely to expound fully all that I understood about light, adding, as the opportunity arose, something about the sun and the fixed stars, from which almost all light proceeds; about the skies, which transmit light; about the planets, the comets, and the earth, which reflect it; in particular, about all terrestrial bodies because they are coloured, or transparent, or luminous; and finally about man because he is the spectator of all this. Indeed, in order to leave all these things a little bit in shadow, and in order to be able to say more freely what my conclusions were, without being obliged either to follow or to refute the opinions commonly held by the learned, I resolved to leave all these people to their quarrels, and to talk only about what would happen in a new world, if God were to create now, somewhere in the imaginary spaces, enough matter to compose it, and if He were to agitate the various parts of this matter in such a way as to engender a chaos as full of confusion as the poets can imagine, and if, thereafter, He were to do no more than sustain nature, and leave it to act according to the laws He has established.

First, then, I described this matter, and tried to show that, apart from what I have already said about God and the soul, there is nothing, as it seems to me, clearer or more intelligible in the world; and for this purpose I argued expressly that it had none of those forms or qualities that are debated in the Schools, nothing, in fact, of which the knowledge was not so natural to our minds that we could not even pretend to be ignorant of it. I also showed what the laws of nature were; and, without basing my argument on anything but the infinite perfections of God, I endeavoured to prove all those laws of which there could be any doubt, and to show that they were such that, even if God had created many worlds, there could not be one in which the same laws were not observed. Next, I showed how the greatest part of the matter of this chaos must, in accordance with these laws, so arrange and dispose itself as to resemble our skies, and how some of the remaining parts constitute an earth, others the planets and comets, and others still, a sun and fixed stars. And, at this point, expatiating on the subject of light, I explained at length what kind of light is to be found in the sun and in the stars, how from them it traverses the vast expanse of the skies in an instant, and how it is reflected from the planets and comets to the earth. To all this I added many details concerning the substance, the location, the movements, and the different qualities of the skies and the heavenly bodies, and I thought that, in this way, I had said enough to make known that there was nothing in all that constitutes this world that should not, or at least could not, seem exactly similar to what constituted the world I was describing.

I next spoke of the earth in detail, noting how, even though I had expressly laid it down that God had put no quality of heaviness into the matter of which it is composed, all its parts tend constantly towards its centre; how, as there is air and water on its surface, the disposition of the skies and of the heavenly bodies must cause an ebb and flow similar in all respects to what we observe in our seas, as well as certain currents of both air and water, running from west to east, such as may be noticed in the tropics; how mountains and seas, springs and rivers, can develop naturally, how metals can appear in the mines, and plants grow in the fields, and, in general, how the bodies we call mixed or composite can be engendered. Among other things, and because I know of nothing else besides the heavenly bodies (except fire) that produces light, I took pains to explain clearly all that belongs to its nature, how it appears, and how it spreads; how it sometimes has heat without light, and sometimes light without heat; how it introduces different colours into different bodies, with various other characteristics; how it melts certain bodies, and hardens others; how it can consume almost all bodies and convert them into cinders and smoke; and how, finally, it can, by the violence of its action, transmute cinders into glass; for, as the transmutation of cinders into glass seems to me more wonderful than anything else that happens in nature, I took particular pleasure in describing it.

However, I do not wish to infer from all this that this is the way in which God created the world; it is much more likely that He made it, from the first, as it is now. What is certain is that it is the opinion commonly held by the theologians that the act by which He keeps it now in existence is identical with the act by which He created it. And so, although He may have made it a chaos in the first instance, we may believe that, provided He had established the laws of nature and sustained nature itself in acting according to custom, all purely material things would, in the course of time, have assumed the form in which we see them today, without this belief being a slight upon the miracle of creation. Indeed, the nature of material things is easier to conceive when we see them develop little by little than when we only consider them as fully formed.

From the description of inanimate bodies and plants I went on to the description of animals, and particularly of men. As, however, I lacked the knowledge to speak of the latter in the same way as of the rest, that is to say, by proving effects by their causes, and by showing how, and from what elements, nature must produce them, I contented myself with supposing that God shaped man's body as exactly similar to ours, with exactly the same conformation of external limbs, making it of the same matter as I have described above, and without placing in him, at the beginning, any rational soul, nor anything that might serve as an animal or vegetable one, but merely kindling in his heart the kind of fire without light I had already explained, which I took to be the kind of fire which heats hay, when it has been piled up before it is dry, or which causes new wine to seethe, when it has been left to ferment on the lees. For, when I examined what functions there could consequently be in such a body, I found precisely those we can have without our thinking of them, and without the soul (that part of us distinct from the body whose whole nature it is, as I have said, to think) being called upon to make any contribution. And I was unable to discover any of those functions which, being dependent upon thought, alone belong to us as men, whereas I discovered them all later on, once I had supposed that God had created a rational soul and had joined it to the body in a manner which I described.

In order, however, to let people see how I treated the whole subject in my book, I wish here to give an account of the movement of the heart and the arteries, which is the first and the chief thing we look at in animals; and it will be easy from this account to judge the value of the rest of my explanations. But first, in order that he should have less difficulty in following my words, I should like any reader unversed in anatomy to take the trouble to have the heart of some large animal with lungs dissected in front of him, for the heart of an animal is very like that of a man, and to be shown the two chambers or cavities[1] that are found in it.

First, let him observe the cavity to the right to which are attached two very large tubes, namely, the *vena cava* which is the principle receptacle of the blood and is like the trunk of the tree of which all the other veins in the body are like branches, and the arterial vein[2] (ill-named,

1. Left ventricle and right ventricle.   2. Pulmonary artery.

because it is in effect an artery) which originates in the heart and then divides, when it has left the heart, and spreads into several branches through the lungs. Then there is the left-hand cavity to which are attached in the same way two other tubes, as thick as the former ones, or even thicker, namely, the veinous artery[1] (ill-named, because it is really a vein) which comes from the lungs, and is divided into several branches interlaced with the branches of the arterial vein and with those of the wind-pipe[2] (as it is called) through which we breathe, and the grand artery[3] which, coming out of the heart, disperses its branches throughout the body.

Let the reader also observe carefully the eleven pelli-cules which are like so many little doors opening and closing the four entrances to these two cavities.[4] Three of these little doors are disposed at the mouth of the *vena cava* in such a way that they cannot prevent the blood from flowing into the right-hand cavity, and yet prevent it very effectively from flowing out; three others,[5] at the mouth of the arterial vein, are so placed, on the contrary, that they allow the blood in the left-hand cavity to flow into the lungs, but do not allow it to return; in the same way, two other little doors,[6] at the mouth of the veinous artery, allow the blood from the lungs to flow into the left-hand cavity, but do not allow it to flow back; the last three doors,[7] at the mouth of the grand artery, allow the blood to flow out of the heart, but prevent its returning. And there is no need to seek an explanation of the number of pellicules in anything else but the fact that the opening into the grand artery, being oval because of its situation, can comfortably be closed by two doors, while, as the other openings are round, three doors are more effective.

1. Pulmonary vein. 2. Trachea. 3. Aorta.
4. Tricuspid valve. 5. Sigmoid valve. 6. Bicuspid valve.
7. Sigmoid valve at the mouth of the aorta.

Let it also be observed that the grand artery and the arterial vein are of a much harder and firmer texture than the veinous artery and *vena cava*; that the two last swell before they enter the heart, and form, as it were, two little pouches which are called the ears of the heart,[1] and which are of the same composition as they are. Let it be observed, further, that there is always more warmth in the heart than in any other part of the body; and, finally, that this warmth is capable of making every drop of blood that enters the cavities of the heart promptly swell and dilate, just as liquids generally do when they are poured, drop by drop, into some well-heated receptacle.

I can now explain the movement of the heart in a few words. First, when the two cavities are not full of blood, some flows necessarily from the *vena cava* into the left cavity, and some from the arterial vein into the right cavity, especially as these two vessels are always full of blood and their mouths, which open into the heart, cannot be blocked. As soon, however, as two drops of blood have entered the heart, these drops, which are very thick because the openings through which they penetrate are very wide, and the vessels from which they come very full, rarefy and dilate, because of the heat they find in the heart, and so, making the heart swell, they push against and close up the five little doors at the mouths of the two vessels from which they come, and prevent any more blood from flowing into the heart. Then, becoming more and more rarefied, they push open the six other little doors at the mouths of the two vessels by which they flow out, thus causing all the branches of the arterial vein and the grand artery to swell almost at the same time as the heart.[2] Immediately after, the heart deflates[3] as do these arteries, because the blood that has entered them has grown cold, and the six little doors close up again, while

1. Auricles. 2. Diastole. Descartes is here in error. 3. Systole.

the five others of the *vena cava* and the veinous artery re-
open to allow the passage of two more drops of blood
which immediately cause the heart and the arteries to
dilate as before. And it is because the blood that enters
the heart in this way passes through the two little pouches[1]
which are called its ears, that their movement is contrary
to that of the heart, and they deflate as the heart inflates.
Finally, so that those who do not understand the force of
a mathematical demonstration, and are not accustomed to
distinguishing between true reasons and what is merely
plausible, should not take the risk of denying all this
without consideration, I wish to warn them that the
movement I have just explained follows as necessarily
from the mere disposition of the organs the naked eye
can perceive in the heart, from the warmth in it which
can be felt with the fingers, and from the nature of the
blood which can be known by experiment, as the movement of a clock follows from the force, the position, and
the disposition of its counterweights and wheels.

But if one asks how it is that the blood from the veins,
flowing continually into the heart, is never exhausted, and
how it is that the arteries are never too full, since all the
blood that passes through the heart flows into them, I
need give no other reply than that of an English doctor[2]
who must be praised for having broken the ice on this
subject. He is the first to teach that there are several little
exits at the extremities of the arteries through which the
blood that comes from the heart flows into the branched
veins, and immediately flows back to the heart, so that
its whole course is a perpetual circulation. And he proves
this very well by reference to the normal practice of
surgeons who, by binding an arm with moderate force
above the vein they open, cause the blood to flow out
more abundantly than if they had not bound the arm;
whereas the contrary would happen if they were to bind

1. Auricles.　　2. Harvey.

the arm, either below the vein, or very strongly above it. For it is obvious that a tourniquet of moderate tightness, while it can prevent the blood already in the arm from flowing back towards the heart through the veins, does not thereby prevent fresh blood from flowing from the arteries, these being situated below the veins, and being of a harder texture than the veins, and so less affected by pressure; also the blood from the heart tends to pass with greater force through the arteries towards the hand than to flow back from there through the veins towards the heart. Furthermore, as the blood comes out of the arm through an opening in one of the veins, there must be certain openings in the arteries below the tourniquet and towards the hand, that is to say, towards the extremities of the hand through which it can flow from the arteries. Our doctor further proves very well his theory of the flow of the blood by pointing to various pellicules disposed in such a way in various places along the veins that they do not allow the blood to flow through the middle of the body towards the extremities, but only from the extremities towards the heart; and there is the further fact we know from experience that all the blood in the body can be drained away very quickly through a single cut artery, even though it should be very tightly bound as close as possible to the heart, and the artery should be cut between the heart and the place where it is bound, so that one has no reason to imagine that the blood comes from anywhere else.

But there are several other things that bear witness to the fact that the true cause of the movement of the blood is as I have said. There is, first of all, the difference between the blood from the veins and the blood from the arteries which can only be due to the fact that the blood is rarefied and, as it were, distilled in passing through the heart, and is therefore thinner, more rapid, and warmer, as it leaves the heart, that is to say, in the arteries, than it was a little while before, that is to say, in the veins. Besides, careful investigation shows that this difference is more apparent in parts near the heart than in those that are distant from it.

Then, the hardness in texture of the arterial vein and the grand artery show clearly that the blood beats in them with greater force than in the veins. And why should the left cavity of the heart and the grand artery be less capacious than the right cavity and the arterial vein? There can be only one reason, and that is that the blood in the veinous artery, having only been in the lungs, after passing through the heart, is thinner and more easily rarefied than the blood which comes immediately from the *vena cava*. What could doctors hope to learn by feeling the pulse, if they did not know that, as the blood changes, it can be more or less strongly, and more or less quickly, rarefied by the warmth of the heart than before. If we enquire how this warmth is communicated to the limbs, must we not admit that it is by means of the blood which, passing through the heart, is re-heated and spreads through the whole body? Hence it is that, by draining the blood from any part of the body, we deprive it at the same time of its warmth; and the heart might be like a brazier, but it would not suffice to warm our hands and feet, as it does, if the blood in them were not constantly renewed.

We see, in the same way, that the true use of breathing is to bring enough fresh air into the lungs so that the blood that flows into it from the right cavity of the heart, where it has been rarefied, and changed, as it were, into vapour, should immediately thicken into blood again before entering the left cavity; otherwise it would furnish no fuel for the fire in the heart. This is confirmed by the fact that animals without lungs have only one cavity in the heart, and that children in the womb, who cannot breathe fresh air, have an opening by which the blood flows into the left cavity of the heart, and a conduit by which it passes from the arterial vein into the grand artery without going through the lungs.

Digestion, too, would be impossible in the stomach if warmth did not reach it from the heart through the arteries, with some of the most fluid blood, and this helps to dissolve the food. It is also easy to understand how the food-juices are converted into blood by a process of distillation of the blood, as it passes in and out of the heart more than a hundred or two hundred times a day. And we need no other explanation of nutrition, and of the various humours we find in the body, than the force with which the blood, as it rarefies, flows towards the extremities of the arteries, and which causes the corpuscles to mingle with those it finds in various parts of the body, while driving out others to take their place, and also causes them to seek out different places, according to the position, shape, or smallness of the pores they encounter, just as different kinds of grain are sorted out by sieves with holes of different sizes.

But what is most remarkable in all this are the animal spirits which resemble the most tenuous of vapours, or rather extremely pure and lively tongues of flame, and which, rising constantly from the heart to the brain, descend from there through the nerves to the muscles, and give movement to the limbs; and we need not suppose any reason why certain corpuscles which, as being the most active and the most penetrating, are the most apt to compose these spirits, move towards the brain rather than elsewhere, except that they are carried thither by the arteries which come most directly from the heart. For, according to the laws of mechanics, which are identical with the laws of nature, when many things tend all together towards a place which is not large enough to contain them all, just as the corpuscles flowing from the left cavity of the heart all tend towards the brain, the feebler and less active are ousted by the others which reach their destination alone.

All this I explained in the treatise it had once been my intention to publish. And I had then shown what the structure of the nerves and muscles of the human body must be in order that the animal spirits within should have the power to make the limbs move; as we see a severed head continue to move and to bite the ground, even though it is no longer animate. I had also shown what must occur in the brain to cause wakefulness, sleep, and dreams; how through the senses it received the ideas of light, sound, smell, taste, warmth, and indeed of all the other qualities of external objects; how it is affected by hunger, thirst, and the other internal feelings; and what there is in it which must be regarded as the common sense which receives all these ideas. Then there was the memory which preserved these ideas, and the imagination which could change them in different ways and make up new ones, and which could, as the animal spirits are distributed through the muscles, cause the limbs of this body to move in as many different ways, according to the variety of sense-perception and internal feelings, as our bodies can move automatically without the intervention of the will. Nor will this seem in any way strange to those who, knowing the different kinds of *automata*, or moving machines, that the industry of men can fabricate with the use of very few parts in comparison with the mass of bones, muscles, nerves, arteries, veins, and so on, which are to be found in the body of every animal, will consider this body as a machine which, as it comes from the hands of God, is far better ordered, with a far more wonderful movement, than any machine that man can invent.

I had also made a special effort to show that, if there were such machines which had the organs and appearance of a monkey, or some other animal, we should have no way of recognizing that they were not entirely of the same nature as these animals, but that, if there were any machines that resembled our own bodies, and imitated our actions as much as possible, we should still have two certain ways of knowing that they were not real men. The first is that they would be unable to put together words, or any other signs, as we do, to utter our thoughts. For we can certainly conceive of a machine so constructed that it can utter words, and can even utter words in relation to bodily actions that cause some change in its organs. Thus, if we touch it in one spot, it may ask us what we want with it; if we touch it in another, it may cry out that it is being hurt, and so on. What it cannot do is to arrange its words in varying ways so as to reply sensibly to whatever is said in its presence, as the stupidest of men can do.

The second reason is that, although these machines might do many things as well as we do them, or even better than we do them, they would inevitably fail with others, whereby we should discover that what they did, they did, not through knowledge, but by the disposition of their organs. For the reason is a universal instrument which can be adapted to all sorts of occasions, but these organs have need of some particular disposition for each particular action. Hence it is in practice impossible to conceive of enough diversity of behaviour in a machine to make it act in all the circumstances of life in the way in which our reason makes us act.

Now these two arguments also make us understand the difference there is between men and animals. It is very remarkable that there are no men, however dull-witted and stupid, without excepting even imbeciles, who are incapable of putting words together and composing some sort of expression of their thoughts, while, on the contrary, there is no animal, however perfect and happily nurtured, capable of doing the same. Nor is this due to the lack of the necessary organs, for magpies and parrots can utter words, as we do. What they cannot do is to speak, as we speak, that is to say, by showing that their words express their thoughts. On the other hand, men who are born deaf and dumb, and lack those organs which serve others, including animals, for the utterance of words, are in the habit of inventing signs which are understood by those who, being often in their company, have the time to learn their language.

And this does not only show that animals have less reason than men; it shows that they have none at all. For it requires very little reason, as we see, to be able to speak; and, as we observe as much inequality between animals of the same species as we see among men, so that some are more easily trained than others, it is incredible that a monkey or a parrot, each among the most perfect of its kind, should not prove the equal of the stupidest child, or even of one with a defective brain, were it not that they have souls of an entirely different nature from ours. Nor should we confound speech with those natural movements which bear witness to the feelings, and which can be imitated by machines as well as by animals, or think, with the ancients, that animals speak, although we do not understand their language. If this were so, since they have many organs which are very like ours, they could make us understand them as well as their fellows. And it is a very remarkable fact that, while many show more industry than we do in some actions, they show none in many others, and so what they do better than we do does not prove that they have any intelligence. If it did, it would also show that they had more intelligence than any one of us, and they would do better in everything. But the fact is that it shows that they have no intelligence at all, and that it is nature working in them according to the disposition of their organs. Thus a clock, composed only of wheels and springs, can count the hours and measure the time more accurately than we can, for all our foresight.

After all this, I had described the rational soul and shown that it cannot by any means be derived from matter, as is the case with the other things I had spoken about, but must be specially created; and I had shown how it was not lodged in the human body, like a pilot in his ship, except perhaps for the purpose of causing the movement of the limbs, but must be more joined and united with the body so as to have, besides, feelings and appetites like ours, and thus constitute a real man. I spent some time on the subject of the soul, because it is one of the most important, and because, after the error of those who deny God, an error I think I have adequately refuted, there is nothing that leads weak minds further astray from the path of virtue than to imagine that the souls of animals are of the same nature as ours, and that, after this life, we have nothing to fear, and nothing to hope, any more than flies and ants; but, when we know how great the difference is, we understand much better that ours is by nature entirely independent of the body, and consequently not subject to dying with it. Then, as we see no other reason for the destruction of the soul than the death of the body, we are led naturally to conclude that the soul is immortal.

6

[*Descartes had laid aside his treatise on the physical universe out of deference to people whose authority he did not wish to question, even though he was himself unaware of holding any views subversive of religion or the state. In any case he has no love of authorship, and there is nothing he wishes to avoid so much as controversy, which would destroy his freedom to pursue his own thoughts. Everyone, however, has laid upon him the duty of procuring, if he can, the good of his fellow men, and Descartes, having discovered much that would*

*benefit mankind, particularly if he were to continue his researches in
medicine, the most generally beneficial of the sciences, has thought that
he must give some inkling of his achievement so far. Above all, he is
in need of help towards the cost of the many and varied experiments
he still requires to make in order to complete his work. But he has
no desire for honours: those will serve him best who will ensure his
independence.*]

IT is now three years since I completed the treatise which
contains all these things, and I had begun to review it
with a view to putting it into the hands of a printer, when
I learned that certain persons to whom I defer, and whose
authority governs my actions no less than my reason
governs my thoughts, had expressed their disapproval
of a theory in physics previously stated by someone else.
I would not say that I held the same theory, although I
had seen nothing in it, before this censure, which seemed
to me prejudicial to religion or to the state, and nothing,
consequently, to prevent me from stating it myself, if my
reason persuaded me to do so; but the incident made me
fear that there might be something in my own views
about which I was under a misapprehension, despite the
great care I have always taken never to admit the truth
of any new opinion without certain proof, and never to
write anything which might harm anyone. It was enough,
however, to make me change my mind about publishing
my book. For, although I had had strong reasons in
favour of my previous resolution, my own inclination,
which has always been to hate the whole business of
writing books, made me immediately find other reasons
to excuse my failure to keep this resolution. And these
reasons are of such a kind, both for and against my first
decision, that it is to my interest to mention them here,
as it may be to the interest of the public to know what
they are.

I have never taken much stock by my own opinions,
and as long as the only fruits of the method I employ were

my own satisfaction with regard to the solution of certain difficulties in the speculative sciences, and as long as I merely regulated my conduct according to the precepts of this method, I thought myself under no obligation to write anything. For in what concerns human behaviour everyone is so ready to expatiate on his own personal opinions that we might have as many reformers as there are heads to think out schemes, were it not that God has given permission only to those whom He has appointed as rulers over His people, or upon whom He has bestowed sufficient grace and zeal to become prophets, to undertake to make any change in our ways. Thus, although my own speculations pleased me a great deal, I thought others might have their own, which pleased them even more. As soon, however, as I had acquired certain general notions in physics, and as soon as I had seen, after putting them to the test in dealing with various particular difficulties, how far they could lead, and how much they differed from the principles hitherto in use, I thought I could not keep them to myself without greatly sinning against the law which enjoins upon us the duty of procuring, as well as we can, the general good of mankind.

For they have made me see that it is possible to reach a kind of knowledge which will be of the utmost use to men, and that in place of that speculative philosophy which is taught in the Schools, we can achieve a practical one by means of which, by ascertaining the force and action of fire, water, the air, the heavenly bodies, and the skies, of all the physical things that surround us, as distinctly as we know the various trades of our artisans, we can apply them in the same way to all the uses for which they are fit, and thus make ourselves, as it were, the lords and masters of nature.

And this is desirable not only for the invention of countless means of enjoying the fruits of the earth and all the good things it contains, but principally for the preservation of health, which is no doubt the chief of all goods and the foundation of all the rest in this life; for even the mind is so dependent on the temperament and the bodily organs that, if a way can be found of making men wiser and more skilful than they have so far proved, I believe we must look for it in medicine. It is true that what is at present practised under that name has little that is of any notable use; and I have no desire to be scornful, but I am sure there is no one, even among those whose profession it is, who would not admit that all we know of it is almost nothing in comparison with what remains to be known, and that we might be liberated from a number of disorders, both of mind and body, and perhaps also from the feebleness of old age, if we had a sufficient knowledge of the causes of these ills, and of all the remedies which nature has provided. Now, as I propose to spend the rest of my life in the search for so necessary a science, and as I have found the road which, if it is followed, must infallibly lead to success, unless the way is blocked by the shortness of life or a dearth of experiments, I judged that the best way of overcoming these two obstacles was by faithfully communicating to the public all I had so far discovered, little though it be, and by inviting men of good will and wisdom to try to go further by contributing, each according to his inclination and power, to the experiments that are required, and also by communicating to the public all they learn. Thus, with the last ones beginning where their predecessors had stopped, and a chain being formed of many individual lives and efforts, we should go forward all together much further than each one would be able to do by himself.

I even observed, regarding these experiments, that they become more necessary the further one's knowledge goes. At the beginning, it is better to make use of what presents itself spontaneously to our senses, and cannot be unknown to us, provided we reflect upon it to some extent, rather than look for what is rarer and more complex, the reason being that what is rare is often deceptive when we are still unaware of the most ordinary causes, and that the circumstances on which the former depend are almost always so special and so slight that it is very difficult to distinguish them. But the order I have observed in all my researches is the following. First, I have sought to discover in general the principles and first causes of all that exists, or can exist in the world, without taking into consideration, for this purpose, anything but God alone who has created the world, and only drawing upon certain elements of truth which inhabit our minds. After this, I took note of the effects which immediately and most commonly follow upon these causes, and so I discovered, as it seems to me, the skies, the heavenly bodies, an earth, and, on the earth itself, water, air, fire, minerals, and such other things which, being the commonest and the simplest, are the easiest to understand. When, however, I attempted a more detailed survey, I found such a diversity of objects to consider that I did not think it possible for the human mind to distinguish the kinds or species of bodies that inhabit the earth from an infinite number of others that might have existed, if God had so willed it; nor do I think it possible to turn all this to our use, except by looking for the cause through the effect, and by conducting a large number of special experiments.

Then, going over in my mind all the objects perceived by my senses, I dare to affirm that there was nothing I could not explain comfortably enough, by the principles I had discovered. On the other hand, I must confess that the power of nature is so ample and so vast, and these principles are so general, that I no longer observe almost any particular effect but I see immediately that it can be deduced from these principles in a number of different ways. And the only expedient I know of then is to try a number of experiments so contrived as to vary the result, with the object of seeing how the effect is to be explained. I have now reached the point where I see well enough, as it seems to me, how to go about most of these experiments; but I also see that they are of such a kind, and so numerous, that neither the work of my hands, nor my income, even if it were a thousand times what it is, would suffice for all of them; and I shall make more or less progress in the knowledge of nature accordingly as I have more or less opportunity for making my experiments. It was this knowledge I had promised myself to divulge in my treatise, showing so clearly its usefulness to the public that I should oblige all those who wish to further the welfare of mankind, all those, in fact, who are really men of virtue, and not virtuous simply in appearance and by repute, both to communicate to me the results of their own experiments and to help me in those that remain to be done.

Since then, other reasons have made me change my mind about publishing my book. I now think I should certainly continue to write down anything of importance according as the truth is revealed to me, and should bring to my writing as much care as if I intended it for the printer. This would give me more opportunity to scrutinize my work, as we always look more closely at what we think is to be seen by many people, and as, very often, what has seemed to me true, when I have done no more than think about it, has seemed to me quite false, when I have set it down on paper. I should also still be able to benefit the public, insofar as I am capable of doing so, since, if my writings are of any value, those into whose hands they fall after my death may make such use of them as they think fit. I was determined, however, never to agree to their being published during my lifetime, lest the opposition and the controversies they might be subjected to, or even the reputation I might acquire, whatever it might prove to be, should cause me to lose the time I propose to devote to my own instruction.

Every man, it is true, lies under the obligation of procuring, as well as he can, the welfare of others, and to be of no use to anyone is properly to be worth nothing; but it is also true that our preoccupations should extend beyond the present, and it is right to omit to do what may benefit our contemporaries, when the intention is to benefit posterity still more. I am very willing to confess that the little I have learned is as nothing compared to what I do not know, but do not despair of learning. For it is with the acquisition of truth in the sciences as with the acquisition of riches. The wealthy have less trouble in making vast gains than they had, when they were poor, in making much smaller ones. In the same way, the leaders of armies are accustomed to see their forces grow in proportion to their victories, and require more skill in defending their position after a defeat than in capturing towns and provinces after a victory. And it is truly to give battle to attempt the conquest of all those difficulties and errors that prevent us from attaining to the knowledge of the truth, just as it is a defeat when we accept a false opinion in a matter of some general importance; we then require more skill to recover our position than we need for making great progress when our principles are assured.

For myself, if I have already discovered a few truths in the sciences (and I think that the essays[1] contained in this volume will allow it to be thought that I have discovered some), I can say that they merely follow and depend upon the overcoming of five or six principal difficulties, and I count these victories as the winning of so many battles in which fortune has been on my side. I

1. As has been pointed out in the Introduction, the *Discourse on Method* was originally published as a preface to three essays.

would even make so bold as to say that I need only to win two or three more similar encounters in order to reach my goal, and that I am not so far advanced in age, according to the normal course of nature, not to have the time for my purpose. I think, however, that I am all the more obliged to use my time cautiously as I have more hope of using it to advantage, and I should no doubt have many opportunities of wasting it if I published my treatise on the foundations of physics. For, although my basic notions are almost all so evident that they need only be understood to be believed, and there is none I do not think I can demonstrate, yet because it is impossible that they should be in accord with the various opinions of others, I fear I should often be distracted from my main task by the opposition they would arouse.

It can be said that this opposition would be of use, both in making me recognize my mistakes, and in order that, where I am right, others should understand me better, and also that, as many can see more than a single person can, they should, by beginning to make use of what I have found, help me with their own discoveries. However, although I know that I am extremely subject to error, and almost never rely upon my first notions, the experience I have had of the objections put forward to my views prevents me from expecting any benefit from them. I have been the object of many judgements from various sources, from those whom I held to be my friends, from some to whom I thought I was indifferent, and even from others whose malice and envy would, I knew, seek to lay bare what affection might conceal from my friends; but I have rarely encountered any objection to my views from any source which I had altogether failed to foresee, unless it happened to be quite irrelevant to my theme. I have, thus, almost never met with any censor of my opinions who has not seemed to me either less rigorous, or less equitable, than myself; nor have I observed that the set debates which are customary in the Schools[1] have ever served towards the discovery of a single new truth. On the contrary, as each one struggles for the victory, more care is taken in advocating what is plausible, than in weighing the reasons put forward on either side: good lawyers do not necessarily make the best judges.

As for the usefulness of my thoughts to others, this cannot be very considerable, since I have not carried them to the point where there would be little to add before they could be put into practice. And I think I may say, without vanity, that, if there is anyone capable of reaching this point, it must be myself rather than another. Not that there may not be in the world many minds incomparably superior to mine, but that one cannot conceive a thought so well, and make it one's own, by learning it from another, as when one discovers it oneself. And this is so true, in the subject under discussion, that I have often had occasion to explain my opinions to men of very good mind who seemed to understand them quite distinctly, while I was speaking, but who, in repeating them, seemed to me to have changed them in such a way that I could no longer recognize them as my own. And in this connexion, I beg those who come after me never to believe what I am reported to have said unless I have stated it myself. Nor do I wonder at the extravagant sayings attributed to those ancient philosophers whose writings have not come down to us, and I conclude, not that their notions were extremely unreasonable, for they were the best minds of their time, but that they have been misrepresented.

One sees, too, that they have almost never been surpassed by any one of their followers; and I am sure that the most passionately devoted of the followers of

1. Among scholastic theologians and philosophers, e.g. at the Sorbonne.

Aristotle would consider themselves happy if they knew as much about nature as he did, even if it were a condition that they should never know more. But they are like the ivy which never seeks to go higher than the tree which gives it support, and often even turns downwards after it has reached the summit. For these sectaries,[1] too, seem to me to be moving downwards, that is to say, to be making themselves less learned than if they had never studied, for not content with learning from their author all that he has intelligibly expounded, they seek to find in him the solution of problems of which he says nothing, and which had probably never occurred to him. However, this is a very convenient way of philosophizing for those who have only very mediocre minds; for the obscurity of the distinctions and principles they employ is the reason why they make bold to speak about everything as if they knew it, and to maintain their opinions against the most subtle and the most skilful, without there being any means of convincing them that they are wrong. But in all this they make me think of a blind man who, in order to battle on even terms with a man who can see, entices his opponent into the depths of a very dark cellar; and I may affirm that it is to the interest of these philosophers that I should abstain from publishing my philosophical principles; for, as these are very simple and very evident, I should be doing the same, by giving them to the public, as if I were to open a few windows and let the daylight into the cellar into which our philosophers have descended in order to do battle.

Even the best minds need have no desire to become acquainted with my principles. If what they want is to be able to talk on all subjects, and to acquire the reputation of being learned men, they will succeed more easily by contenting themselves with the plausible, which can be discovered in all sorts of matters without much trouble,

1. The Scholastics.

than by looking for the truth, which only reveals itself little by little to a few people, and which when something new arises, obliges us frankly to confess our ignorance. On the other hand, if they prefer the knowledge of a few truths, as no doubt they should, to the vanity of appearing ignorant of nothing, and if they wish to pursue a design similar to mine, they do not need to be told anything more than I have said in this discourse. For, if they are capable of going further than I have, they are still more capable of discovering for themselves all that I think I have discovered, especially as, having examined nothing here except in order, what I still have to find is certainly in itself more difficult and more recondite than anything I have hitherto encountered, and they would have far less pleasure in learning it from me than for themselves. Besides, the habit they will acquire of beginning with easy things, and going on by degrees to the more difficult, will be of greater use to them than all my instructions could be. As for myself, I am convinced that, if I had been taught in my youth all those truths I have since sought to demonstrate, and had had no trouble in learning them, I should perhaps never have known any others; at least, I should never have acquired the habit and facility, which I think I have, of finding fresh truths, accordingly as I set myself to look for them. In a word, if there is any sort of task in the world that cannot be better accomplished than by the one who has begun it, it is the task on which I am engaged.

It is true that for the experiments required a single person would not suffice, but he could usefully employ no other hands but his own, except those of artisans, or of such people as could be paid for their labour, who would be urged on by the hope of gain, a most effective stimulus, to do exactly everything he should prescribe. Volunteers, on the other hand, who might offer him their help, from curiosity, or with a desire to learn, usually promise more than they achieve, and make proposals which never come to anything; and they would inevitably wish to be rewarded by the solution of certain problems, or at least by compliments and useless conversations, which, however little time they took up, would still be a waste of it. As for the experiments conducted by others, even if they were willing to communicate them to him, as those who think of them as secrets would never do, they are usually compounded of so much that is superfluous that he would find it far from easy to disentangle the particle of truth they contain. Besides, he would find almost all these experiments so badly explained, or so full of error, because those who have performed them have struggled to make them appear to be in conformity with their principles, that it would not be worth his while to spend any time in picking out those that might be useful. Thus, if there were anyone in the world who should be capable of making the greatest and most useful discoveries, and who should, for this reason, be aided by others in every way, and with every effort, for the achievement of his purpose, I do not see how they could help him better than by defraying the costs of the experiments he needs to make, and also by safeguarding his time from the importunity of anyone. For my part, I am not so presumptuous as to wish to promise anything out of the ordinary, nor do I feed my mind on such empty fancies as to suppose that the nation should take much interest in my projects; but I am not so poor-spirited as to be willing to accept any favour from anyone which I may not be thought to have deserved.

All these considerations, taken together, constituted the reason why, three years ago, I was unwilling to publish the treatise I had ready; I was even resolved to divulge no other work during my lifetime which should be on such general lines and should make known the foundations of my physics. Since then, however, there have been two reasons to compel me to collect the essays contained in this volume and to give the public some account of my actions and projects. The first reason is that, if I failed to do so, many who knew that it had formerly been my intention to have some of my work printed, might imagine that my reasons for not doing so were less creditable than they are. For, although I have no excessive love of glory, which I may even say I hate insofar as I judge it inimical to seclusion, which I esteem above everything else, I have also never attempted to conceal my actions as if they were crimes, nor taken many precautions to remain unknown, both because I thought it would do me an injustice, and because it would have caused a sort of anxiety immediately prejudicial to that ease of mind that I desire. Then, although quite indifferent as to whether I were known or not, I have not been able to prevent myself from acquiring a certain reputation, so that I thought I should do my best to preserve myself from getting a bad one. The second reason why I have written this volume is that, in view of the delay in my task of discovery, owing to the vast number of experiments which I require to make, and which I cannot achieve without help from others, and although I do not flatter myself so much as to hope that the public should be greatly interested in my affairs, I do not wish to fail in my duty towards myself and so give those who survive me some grounds for complaining of me that I might have bestowed upon them a greater heritage of discoveries, if I had not neglected to inform them how they could assist me in my task.

I also thought it would be easy for me to choose certain subjects which, without being highly controversial and without forcing me to reveal more of my principles than I desired to do, would show, nevertheless, how much I can or cannot do in the sciences. I cannot tell, of course, if I have succeeded in my aim, and I do not wish to influence anyone's judgement in advance by speaking of my writings; but I shall be glad if these are scrutinized, and, in order to encourage people to do so, I shall be glad if those who have any objections to put forward will send them to me through my publisher, and, after I have seen them, they will be published later with my replies, so that others, seeing them together, may more easily judge the truth for themselves. I do not promise that my replies will be very long ones, but I promise to confess my errors freely, when I perceive them, and, when I do not, to argue simply, with such reasons as seem to me required, in defence of what I have written, without introducing any explanation of anything new so as not to be involved in an endless discussion.

Now if some of my remarks at the beginning of the Essays on Dioptrics and on Meteors[1] shock the reader, because I speak of suppositions and seem to have no desire to prove them, let him have the patience to read on with attention, and I hope he will be satisfied. For it seems to me that my reasons follow each other in such a way that, as the last depend upon the first, which are their causes, the first depend upon the last, which are their effects. And it must not be imagined that I am committing the error which logicians call arguing in a circle. For, as most of the effects are quite certain in themselves, the causes from which I deduce them serve rather to explain them than to prove their existence. I have spoken of suppositions because I wish people to know that I think I can deduce them directly from the first truths I have expounded above; but I have deliberately decided to omit such a deduction here in order to prevent minds of a certain stamp, who think they can know in a day what it has taken another twenty years to think out, as soon as he has told them two or three words about it, and who are the more subject to error, and the less

1. Two of the three essays prefaced by the *Discourse on Method*.

capable of the truth, as they are livelier and more penetrating, from taking the opportunity to build up some
philosophical extravaganza on what they think are my
principles, so that their wrong-doing is imputed to me.
As for the opinions that are wholly mine, I do not excuse
them as new. If the reasons on which they are based are
carefully considered, I am sure they will be found to be
so simple and so true to common sense that they will
seem much less strange and much less out of the ordinary
than any other possible opinions on the same subjects.
Nor do I boast of having been the first to invent them,
but only of having accepted them as true, neither because
they have been expressed before, nor because they have
never been expressed before, but simply because my
reason has persuaded me of their truth.

As regards the invention described in the Essay on
Dioptrics, the fact that an artisan should find it difficult
to put it speedily into operation does not mean that it is
a bad invention. So much skill and so much use are
required in assembling the instruments I have described,
so that no detail is missing, that I should be as surprised
to learn that this had been achieved at the first attempt,
as I should be to hear that a person had learned, in a day,
to play like a master on the lute simply by being presented
with a good musical score. And if I have written in
French, the language of my country, rather than in
Latin, the language of my teachers, it is because I hope
that those who make use of their own pure and natural
reason will be better judges of my opinions than those
who believe only in ancient texts. As for those who unite
good sense with learning, and who are the only judges
I wish for, they will not, I am sure, be so enamoured
of Latin as to refuse to understand my reasonings
because I have expressed them in the language of the
people.

And now, to conclude, I do not wish to speak here, in

any detail, of the progress I hope to make in the future in the sciences, nor do I wish to contract any obligation to the public by promising anything I am not sure of achieving. I shall simply say that I am resolved to spend the remaining years of my life in endeavouring to acquire a certain knowledge of nature which will enable me to establish rules of medicine far more assured than we have had so far; and my inclination is so far removed from any other sort of project, and particularly from any occupation which, while being useful to some is harmful to others,[1] that if occasion forced it upon me, I do not think I would be capable of succeeding in it. And so let me make this declaration, that I am well aware that I should not know how to make myself a man of consequence in the world, and also that I have no desire to be one; and I shall always be more obliged to those by whose favour I shall enjoy my seclusion without hindrance than to those who would offer me the most distinguished occupations in the world.

1. Descartes was afraid he might be required to apply his scientific knowledge to the art of war.

Meditations

*

THINGS WE MAY DOUBT

[*The* Discourse on Method *constitutes in effect a training of the mind; the* Meditations *elaborate the philosophical principles briefly set out in the fourth section of the* Discourse. *Descartes does not expound; the* Meditations *are what the title suggests, a concentrated effort of thought bearing upon the existence of the self, of God, and of the external world.*

In order to secure his starting-point, Descartes begins with methodical doubt. It is possible to doubt not only the existence of material things, but the very possibility of knowledge. For God may have so arranged things as to deceive us about what seems most obvious to our minds. But this is a terrifying thought, and the Meditation breaks off at this point.]

MANY years have passed since I first noticed how many false opinions I had accepted as true from my earliest years, and how flimsy a structure I had erected on this treacherous ground; and so I felt that I must one day rid myself of all the opinions I had hitherto adopted, and start the whole work of construction again from the very foundation, if I aspired to make some solid and lasting contribution to knowledge. But this seemed a gigantic task, and I waited until I was of a sufficiently mature age, when no later stage of my life was likely to prove more suitable for my undertaking; and this has made me hesitate so long that any further delay would seem a crime, causing me to waste in deliberation the time left to me for achievement. Now therefore that my mind is happily free of all care, and that I have secured for myself untroubled leisure in a safe retreat, I shall apply myself earnestly and freely to the general overthrow of all my former opinions.

For this purpose, I shall not need to prove them all false, for I might never come to an end of them; but, as my reason has already persuaded me to withhold my assent from whatever is less than indubitable, no less scrupulously than from whatever is plainly false, the slightest suspicion of a doubt will be enough to make me reject any one of my beliefs. Nor will it be necessary for me to scrutinize each one in turn, an unending task; but, as the undermining of the foundations brings about the collapse of the whole superstructure, I shall direct my attack in the first place on the principles upon which my former opinions were based.

Now truth of the most assured kind seems to have come to me hitherto, either directly or indirectly, from my senses. But the senses, in my experience, are sometimes deceptive; and it is but prudent not to trust entirely to those who have once deceived us.

To this it may be objected that, even though our senses sometimes deceive us with regard to barely perceptible or distant things, there are perhaps many other matters about which we can have no reasonable doubt; as, for instance, that I am seated here beside the fire, clad in my dressing gown, with this paper in my hands, and so on. How could I deny that these hands and this body were mine? If I did, I should range myself with those unbalanced wretches whose brains are so troubled and darkened with the black vapours of bile that they constantly call themselves kings, when they are poverty-stricken, assert that they are arrayed in gold and purple, when they are naked, or imagine that they are curved into the shape of pitchers, or have bodies blown out of glass. They are mad, of course, and I should be mad in the eyes of men if I were thought to be following their example.

So much is clear, and yet I must remember that I am a man who sleeps at night, and suffers in his dreams the same experiences as these madmen suffer awake, or sometimes others even less reasonable than theirs. How often has it happened to me to dream at night that I was here, in this place, dressed and seated by the fire, when all the time I was lying naked in my bed. At the moment, certainly, it does not seem to be with the eye of sleep that I am looking at this paper; the head I move is not sunk in slumber; and it is with design and deliberation that I stretch out my hand and feel it. Surely what happens in a dream is not as distinct as all this? But then I remember how often in the past I have been deceived in my sleep by similar illusions, and when I reflect upon the matter more closely, I see so clearly that there are no conclusive signs by which to distinguish between our waking and our sleeping moments, that I am dumbfounded, and my confusion is such that I can almost believe myself asleep at this moment.

Now let us suppose that we are in fact asleep, and that all these particular actions, namely, that we open our eyes, move our heads, and stretch out our hands, are all illusions, and that even these hands, or even this whole body, are not what we see them to be. At least, it must be admitted that the objects which appear to us in sleep are coloured representations which could not be formed except in the likeness of real things; and, consequently, those general entities, such as eyes, a head, hands, and a whole body, exist in reality, and not simply in the imagination. Even painters, who struggle to represent their Sirens and Satyrs in the most unexpected and bizarre shapes, are unable to provide them with entirely novel forms, but must have recourse to compounds of the limbs of various animals. And, if one of them should succeed in devising something so entirely new that nothing like it has ever been seen before, and the object is plainly fictitious and unreal, at least the colours of the composition are to be found in reality.

On the same principle, we may admit that general entities, such as eyes, a head, hands, and so on, can be imaginary; but there are others, still simpler, and even more general, and of these everything we may conceive, whether real or unreal, must be composed, just as real colour enters into the composition of any object. Such universal entities are corporeal nature and its extension; the shape, or figure, of extended things, their quantity, or magnitude, and their number; the space in which these extended things exist, and the time through which they endure, and so on. We may reasonably conclude that physics, astronomy, medicine, and all other sciences which have composite objects, are indeed of a doubtful character, but that arithmetic, geometry, and those sciences which have the simplest and most general objects, without much regard to their real existence, have in them something that is at once certain and indubitable. For, whether I be awake or asleep, two and three always make five, and a square always has four sides; nor does it seem possible that such manifest truths should ever incur the least suspicion of falsehood.

And yet, the belief in an all-powerful God, who has made me what I am, has long inhabited my mind, and who can give me the assurance that this God has not so disposed matters that there should be neither earth nor sky, no extended reality, no figure, no magnitude, and no space, and yet that I should imagine that all these exist just as I seem to perceive them? And I can go further, and just as I judge that others are sometimes in error about matters of which they profess the most perfect knowledge, so too I may be wrong (by God's desire) every time I add two and three together, or count the sides of a square, or perform some even simpler operation of the mind, if any such can be imagined. It may be, of course, that God, who is the sovereign good, does not wish me to be deceived in this way; but if it is contrary to His goodness that I should be deceived all the time, it seems inconsistent that I should be deceived sometimes, and it cannot be said that this does not happen.

There may be some, of course, who would prefer to deny the existence of a God so powerful, than to admit that everything else is uncertain. But let us not argue with them for the moment, and let us suppose that all that has been said here of the Deity is a mere fable. Now, however they choose to explain my existence, whether by fate, or by chance, or as the product of an infinite series of events, or in some other unimagined manner, it is clear that, since error and deception are imperfections, the less powerful they make the author of my being, the more likely it is that I should be so imperfect as to be mistaken all the time. I am not arguing against these people; but what I am forced to admit is that there is nothing I once thought true of which I may not legitimately conceive a doubt, and this not from lack of reflection or from lightness of judgement, but for strong and deeply considered reasons. Henceforth, I must check and suspend my judgement of these notions, and refuse my assent to what I have thought true no less scrupulously than to manifest falsehoods, if I am ever to find certitude in the sciences.

But it is not enough to make these observations; I must take care to have them always in mind; for those old, accustomed opinions constantly recur, as if usage and long familiarity had given them the right to occupy my thoughts, and dominate my mind. And I shall never lose the habit of acquiescing in them, and of giving them my trust, so long as I merely take them for what they are in fact, opinions subject to doubt, as I have shown, but highly probable, which it is much more reasonable to accept than to reject. That is why I think I shall be acting prudently if I take my stand against this tendency of mine, and practise a deception on myself by feigning for a time to believe that all these habitual opinions are false and imaginary, until in the end my old and new prejudices will so balance each other that my mind cannot incline to either side, and perverse customs will no longer overcome my judgement, and turn it aside from the right road to truth.

I will suppose, therefore, that there is no God of goodness, the sovereign source of truth, but a malignant genius, as powerful as he is cunning and deceitful, who has used all his zeal to deceive me; and I will make myself think that the sky, the air, the earth, colours, shapes, and sound, indeed every external thing we perceive, are all no more real than the illusions of dreams, by means of which this Demon has laid traps for my credulity. I will conceive myself as having neither hands nor eyes, neither flesh nor blood, and no senses at all, and yet as falsely believing myself to be possessed of all these things. I shall cling obstinately to this notion and though with its help I may not be able to acquire the knowledge of any truth, it will at least enable me to suspend my judgement. And so I shall be extremely careful not to give my assent to what is false, but to arm my spirit against the wiles of this great deceiver in such a way that, powerful and cunning as he may be, he will never be able to impose upon me.

But this undertaking is arduous, and a certain indolence leads me imperceptibly back to my ordinary way of life. Just as a slave, dreaming happily that he is free, fears to be awakened as soon as he suspects that his freedom is but a dream, and conspires with his delightful illusion to prolong the deceit, so do I fall back unawares into my old opinions, and fear to be roused from my slumber lest the laborious vigils that must follow upon this tranquil rest, so far from bringing light to my mind in its search for truth, should prove inadequate to dispel all the darkness caused by the difficulties that have just been raised.

2

OF THE NATURE OF THE HUMAN MIND, AND THAT IT IS EASIER TO KNOW THAN THE BODY

[Descartes is in a great state of perturbation, on the verge of complete scepticism. He must go on, however, until he is at least sure that there is no certainty to be achieved, or until he finds one impregnable certainty. And he finds it in the cogito ergo sum. *For let me suppose, with Descartes, the existence of a Malicious Demon whose pleasure it is systematically to deceive me about everything, there is one thing he cannot make me doubt, one thing I am clearly and distinctly aware of, and that is my own existence. I may doubt all the evidence of my senses, but it is the mind that knows the truth. It is the mind that recognizes a piece of wax despite all the forms it may take when heat is applied to it. And the mind is easier to know than material things, supposing they exist.]*

YESTERDAY'S Meditation has filled my mind with so many doubts that it is no longer in my power to forget them. And yet I do not see how I shall be able to resolve them. It is as if, fallen unawares into very deep water, I can neither touch bottom with my feet, nor strike out to bear myself up. I shall make the effort, nevertheless, and then follow the road I took last night, leaving behind me everything of which I am able to conceive the slightest doubt; and I shall continue in this way until I have met with some certainty, or at least, if I cannot do otherwise, until I have reached the point at which I know for certain that there is nothing certain in the world.

In order to move the terrestrial globe from its place and transport it to another, Archimedes asked for nothing more than a single fixed and assured point. I shall have the right to entertain great hopes if I am fortunate enough to find one impregnable certainty.

I begin then by supposing that everything I see is false.

I persuade myself that nothing has ever existed of all that my deceptive memory represents to me. I think myself devoid of any senses. I believe that body, figure, extension, movement, and place are all fictions of my mind. What is left that we can think of as true? Perhaps only this, that there is nothing certain in the world.

But how do I know there is not something else, beyond all that I have just condemned as uncertain, about which one could not conceive the least doubt? Perhaps there is a God, or some other power, that puts these thoughts into my mind? No, that is unnecessary, I may be capable of producing them of myself. But then what of myself meanwhile? Am I not something? Here, although I have already denied the existence of my senses and of my body, I pause to consider. For what follows? Am I so dependent on my senses and on my body that I cannot exist without them? In persuading myself that there was nothing at all in the world, neither heaven nor earth, no minds and no bodies, did I not also persuade myself that I did not exist? Certainly not, for there can be no doubt that I exist in the very act of persuading myself, or indeed of thinking anything at all. Suppose, however, there were some extremely powerful and cunning deceiver filled with zeal to trick me. But there is no doubt that I exist in being deceived, and so, let him deceive me as much as he likes, he can never turn me into nothing so long as I think that I am something. Whence, after due thought and scrupulous reflection, I must conclude that the proposition, *I am, I exist,* is true of necessity every time I state it or conceive it in my mind.

I still do not know, however, with sufficient clarity, what I am; and I must be on my guard, therefore, against imprudently taking myself for something other than I am, and thereby going astray in the very knowledge which is, I maintain, the most certain and the most evident of all. And, for this reason, I shall once again reflect upon what I once thought I was, before I came upon these last thoughts, cutting away whatever notions I had which seem invalidated, however slightly, by the reasons I have already put forward, so that nothing may remain but what is solidly certain.

What, then, did I once take myself to be? A man – but what is a man? Shall I say a rational animal? No, for thereafter I shall have to enquire into the meaning first of 'animal', and then of 'rational', and so slip from a single question into a hundred difficulties. I have neither time nor leisure to waste on such subtleties. I will attend, rather, to those motions which came to life in my mind naturally and spontaneously, as often as I turned to consider my own being. I thought of myself, in the first place, as having a face, hands, and arms, that whole machine made up of bones and flesh such as may be discerned even in a corpse, which I called my body. I thought of myself, further, as taking nourishment, moving, sensing, and thinking, all of which actions I referred to my soul; but I did not stop to consider what this soul was or, if I did, I imagined it as something exceedingly tenuous, something like a breath of air, or like a flame, or like a vapour, which permeated all the thickest parts of my body. As for my body itself, I had no doubt that I knew its nature distinctly, and, if I had had to describe it, in accordance with my ideas about it, I should have described it as limited by its particular shape, as circumscribed by its position in space, and as occupying this position in such a way as to exclude all other bodies. I should have explained, further, that it fell within the purview of the senses so that it could be touched, seen, heard, tasted, or smelt, and that it could be moved in various ways by something other than itself from which it received the impulse, although it could not certainly move of its own power; for this power, or the power of sensing, or the power of thinking, formed no part, in my judgement, of the nature of the body. Rather did I wonder that these powers were nevertheless found in certain bodies.

Now, however, that I have supposed the presence of a supremely powerful – and if I dare say it – malignant genius, whose resources and diligence are all directed towards deceiving me, what am I to say? Can I assure myself that I possess even a minimum of all those characteristics that I have attributed to the body according to its nature? I pause to consider the matter attentively. I go over each attribute in my mind, and repeat the process till I am weary. I find no one to which I may lay claim as belonging to me. What about those, then, which I referred back to the soul? Nutrition, for example, and movement? But if I have no body these are but figments. Sensing? Even this is impossible without the body, and I have seen very many things in dreams which I have later understood were not, in fact, perceived by my senses. Lastly, there is thought? And now I have found it; for thought is the one attribute which cannot be wrenched from me. I am, I exist: that is certain. But for how long? For as long as I think. If I ceased to think, I might very well cease to be, or to exist, at that moment. So now I am admitting nothing but what is necessarily true; I am, by definition, a thinking thing[1], that is to say, a mind or soul, an understanding or a rational being, terms of which the meaning has hitherto been unknown to me. I am a real thing, truly existent. What sort of thing? I have already given the answer: a thinking thing. And what else? Let me call upon my imagination. I am not that assemblage of limbs which is called the human body; I am not something tenuous infused into that body; I am not a breath of air, nor a flame, nor vapour, nor breath itself, nothing of all that I can invent with my imagination, since I have supposed that none of all this exists, and

1. See Note on Cartesian Terminology, p. 192.

yet, without abandoning my hypothesis, I am still certain that I am something.

It may be, however, that there are things, whose existence I deny because they are unknown to me, which do not in reality differ from me. I know nothing about that, and that is not the point at issue; I can judge only of what I do know. I have recognized my own existence, and I want to know what that being is whose existence I now know. It is most certain that this knowledge of myself, taken in this precise sense, does not depend upon things of which the existence is still unknown to me, and not, further, upon any of the products of my imagination. And the very word, imagination, warns me of my error. It would be fiction indeed, and nothing real, if I were to imagine myself, for to imagine is nothing more than to contemplate the outward shape or image of some physical thing. Now I know for certain that I exist, and at the same time I know that, taken as a whole, all these images, and in general everything appertaining to bodies, may have no more reality than the figures in a dream. It follows, as I clearly perceive, that it is as unreasonable for me to say: I shall call upon my imagination to inform me more distinctly of what I am, as to say: I am now awake, and I see something real and true, but, because I do not see it distinctly enough, I shall make my business to fall asleep again so that I may see it more truly and with greater evidence in my dreams. Thus I recognize that nothing of all that the imagination can grasp bears any relation to the knowledge I have of myself, and that I must turn away my mind from the workings of the imagination in order to acquire as distinct a perception of my own nature as is possible.

And so, once again, what am I? A thinking thing – a thing, that is to say, which doubts, understands, affirms, denies, wills, and does not will, and which also affirms and feels. This seems a great deal to belong to my nature.

But why should it not? Am I not the same person who doubts almost everything, who understands some things nevertheless and affirms their truth, while denying all the rest, who wants to know many things, but does not want to be deceived, who imagines a good deal, sometimes in spite of himself, and who is aware of a multitude of impressions which seem to arise through his sense-organs? What is there in all this which is not as true as the truth of my own existence, even though I were perpetually asleep, and the one who gives me my existence were doing everything in his power to deceive me? Can any one of these faculties be distinguished from my thought, or described as separate from me? It is so obvious that it is I who doubt, understand, and will, that no further explanation is required. And it is I who imagine, for though chance may have it, as I have already supposed, that everything I imagine is false, the power of imagining still belongs truly to me and to my thought. Finally, it is I who sense or perceive physical things through my senses, I who see the light, hear a noise, and feel heat. But I am asleep you say, and all this is an illusion. Nevertheless, it is I who seem to see, hear, and grow warm: that cannot be an illusion, and that is what is properly called feeling in me. And to feel, in this precise sense, is nothing other than to think. Thus do I begin to know myself, and what I am, a little better than before.

And yet, in spite of all this, I still cannot help thinking that bodies, of which the images are formed by my mind, and which are perceived through my senses, are much more clearly known by me than that something or other in me which my imagination cannot grasp, strange though it seems that I should appear to comprehend what I judge to be infected with doubt and alien to me more distinctly than what I know to be true and to belong to my own nature. But I see what it is; my mind takes pleasure in going astray. Let me then once more give it the reins for a time so that when, later on, at the right moment, these are drawn in again, it may the more easily submit to control.

Let us begin by consideration of the commonest things, those which we think we understand most distinctly, bodies which we touch and see. I am not speaking of bodies in general, for these general motions are usually more confused, but of some particular body. Let us take for example this piece of wax which has just been taken out of the hive; it has not yet lost the sweetness of the honey it contained; it still retains something of the scent of the flowers from which it has been abstracted. Its colour, shape, and size are apparent; it is hard, cold, and tangible, and if you strike it it will give back some sort of sound. Indeed, it has all the characteristics by which a body can be known as distinctly as possible. But now, as I speak, a flame is brought near to it; its lingering savour is dispelled, the scent vanishes, its colour changes, its shape is transformed, its size increases, it turns liquid, it becomes hot, almost too hot to touch, and, though you may knock on it, it will give back no sound. Is it the same wax? It must be confessed that it is; nobody can deny it, no one can think otherwise. Then what was there in it that was so distinctly understood? Certainly, none of those properties which I perceived through my senses; for all that was subject to taste, smell, sight, touch, or hearing has been transformed; and yet the wax remains.

Perhaps then the wax is what I now think it to be, not the sweetness of honey, nor the fragrance of flowers, not its whiteness, shape, or the sound it gave back, but a body which appeared to me under a certain guise, and now reappears under another. But what precisely do I picture to myself when I think of it in this way? Let us consider the matter attentively, and, after subtracting all the characteristics which do not belong to the wax, let us see what remains. Nothing at all except something extended, flexible, and malleable. But what do we mean by flexible and malleable? Does it mean that the wax after having been round is capable of becoming square, and after being square of becoming triangular in shape? No, indeed, it is not that, for I conceive of it as capable of assuming a countless series of shapes, and as my imagination is incapable of embracing such a series, my conception of the wax is not the product of my imagination.

What now is extension? Is it not itself unknown? For it increases as the wax melts, grows even greater when the wax has entirely melted, and much greater still as the heat increases; and I should not conceive of the wax with clarity and truth if I were not aware that it is capable of more variations in extension than I have ever imagined. I must therefore agree that my imagination can in no way conceive what the wax is, but only my understanding. And I speak of this piece of wax in particular; of wax in general it is still more evident. So what is this wax which can only be conceived by my understanding or in my mind? Certainly it is the very object I see, touch, or imagine, and which I knew from the start; but what is to be noticed is that my perception of it is not, and has never been, the product of sight, touch, or imagination, whatever it may have seemed in the first place, but an inspection of the mind, which may well be imperfect and confused as it was before, or clear and distinct as it is now, accordingly as my attention is less or more firmly fixed upon the attributes of which it is composed.

I am taken aback, nevertheless, when I reflect upon the weakness of my mind, and consider how prone it is to error. For, however I may ponder over all this in the silence of my thoughts, words themselves hold me up, and I am almost deceived by the terms of everyday speech. For we say that we *see* the same piece of wax if it is presented to us, and not that we *judge* it to be the same because it has the same colour and the same shape. And from this I would almost conclude that I know the wax by the sight of my eyes, and not by the scrutiny of my mind. If I chance to look out of the window upon the passers-by in the street below, I have no hesitation in saying that I see men, although their hats and cloaks may be no more than a disguise for clockwork figures. Yet I judge them to be truly men; and so, what I thought I saw with my eyes, I really know through the sole power of judgement which resides in my mind.

A man who seeks to raise his understanding above the common level must feel shame at the idea of finding occasions for doubt in the terms of common speech. I prefer to pass beyond them, and to ask myself if I had a more perfect and more evident conception of the wax when I first perceived it, and I thought I knew it only by means of my external senses, or at least by the common sense, as the philosophers call it, than I have now after a more exact enquiry into its nature and into the means by which it can be known. Certainly, it would be ridiculous to feel any doubt. For what was there in the first perception that was clear and distinct, and of which the least animal might not be capable? But when I distinguish between the wax itself and its external qualities, and, just as if I had stripped it of its garments, contemplate it laid bare before me, there may assuredly remain some touch of error in my judgement, but my conception of the wax can only be the conception of a human mind.

Finally, what shall I say of this mind, that is to say, of myself? So far I have admitted nothing in myself save a mind. But what is this self which seems to perceive the wax so distinctly? Do I not know myself, not only with greater truth and certitude, but more distinctly and evidently than I know the wax? And if I judge the wax to exist from the mere fact that I see it, does not my own existence follow more evidently still from the same fact?

For it may well be that what I see is not wax at all; it may even be that I have no eyes with which to see anything; but it cannot be that I who see, or think I see – and I make no distinction henceforth between the two statements – am not something that exists. Similarly, if I judge that the wax exists because I touch it, the same conclusion will follow, namely, that I am. And if my judgement of the wax's existence is due to my imagination, or to any other cause whatsoever, the same conclusion will still follow. Now what I have said of the wax may be said of all the things by which I am surrounded and which are external to me.

Furthermore, if my perception of the wax grows more distinct as it is made known to me, not only by sight and by touch, but in a great variety of other ways, how much more distinctly must I know myself, when all those aids to the perception of the wax, or of some other body, afford even better evidence of the nature of my mind. Besides, there is in the mind itself so much that contributes to its own clarification, that considerations drawn from the perception of bodies hardly deserve to be enumerated.

But now I am spontaneously back at the point I wanted: I now know that our perception of bodies is due neither to the senses nor to the imagination, but solely to the understanding, and that they are known to us not because we see them or touch them, but because we conceive them in thought; and so too I know clearly that there is nothing that can be known to me more clearly and evidently than my own mind.

But the habit of ancient opinions cannot be disposed of so swiftly. I shall do well to pause here, and by meditating at length on these new discoveries in the pursuit of knowledge, imprint them more deeply on my memory.

3

OF GOD, THAT HE EXISTS

[*Thus the next step is to close my mind to all that is not itself, to the senses and to the imagination. The hypothesis that God takes pleasure in deceiving me, I may leave aside for the moment, for I do not know whether there is any God at all. It is a question to be considered, but the right order of enquiry is first to investigate the ideas in my mind. These are of three kinds: innate, adventitious, and fictitious. Fictitious ideas are those I make up myself, like the idea of a griffin. Adventitious ideas are those that seem to emanate from external things through my senses; but I can have no assurance that they are truly representative: is heat the absence of cold, or cold the absence of heat? Some innate ideas are such that I could conceive them of myself, while the idea I have of myself is not in question. There remains the idea of God. I have it in my mind, provided I am attentive to it, and there must be some cause for its existence. But this cause can only be God Himself, for the cause must be adequate to its effect, and it would be absurd to think of a finite being producing of itself the idea of an Infinite Being. The idea of God in my mind is, as it were, the mark of the artisan on his handicraft, and as the God I conceive is Perfection He cannot deceive me.*]

Now I shall close my eyes, stop up my ears, still all my senses, and even the images of physical things I shall either delete from my mind, or, since that can scarcely be done, count them not worth a straw, as being vain and misleading fancies; and so, holding converse only with myself, delving ever deeper within me, I shall endeavour to become little by little better acquainted and more familiar with myself. I am a thinking thing, that is to say, one that doubts, denies, understands a little, is ignorant of a great deal, wills and does not will, and which also imagines and senses. For, as I have already observed, although whatever I sense or imagine is perhaps nothing outside my mind, or in itself, yet these modes of thought, which I call sensation and imagination, reside, I am certain, within me. And, with this brief enumeration, I think I have stated all that I know about myself, little as it is, or all that I have so far discovered.

Now let me ask myself still more diligently whether there may not be something more to learn about myself of which I am still unaware. I am certain that I am a thinking thing; but do I not also know, therefore, what I require in order to be certain of anything? Now this first piece of knowledge yields only a clear and distinct perception of what I affirm, and this would not make me certain of the truth of my statement were it not impossible that anything I perceived so clearly and distinctly could turn out to be false. Hence I am able, as it seems, to lay down the general law that whatever I perceive very distinctly and clearly is necessarily true.

It may be objected that in the past I have accepted as wholly manifest and certain many ideas which I have later recognized to be false. The earth, for example, and the sky, the stars, and in general everything I seized upon through my senses. But what was it I perceived so clearly? Nothing, surely, but the ideas or thoughts which jostled in my mind; and even now I do not deny that those ideas are in me. But there was something else I affirmed, which an habitual credulity made me think I clearly perceived, although I had not done so in fact, and that was that there were things outside my mind from which these ideas emanated and which they exactly resembled. That was where I judged wrongly, or if I happened to judge rightly the truth of my judgement was in no way dependent upon the force of my perception.

On the other hand, when various elementary notions in arithmetic or geometry drew my attention, as that two and three together make five, and so on, did I not conceive them clearly enough to affirm their truth? If, since then, I have considered it possible to cast doubt on such notions, it is only because the thought occurred to me that a God might have given me a nature of such a kind that I should fall into error in the most obvious matters. Thus, as often as this preconceived notion of the sovereign power of God occurs to me, I am constrained to admit that it is easy for such a Being, if He will, so to arrange matters as to make me fall into error even in what presents itself with the clearest possible evidence to my mind. And yet I have only to turn to something I think I perceive very clearly to be so persuaded of its truth that I burst out spontaneously with the words: let him deceive me who will, there is one thing he can never do, and that is to persuade me that I am nothing as long as I think that I am something; or make it appear that I have never existed, it being true that I exist now; or make it true that two and three together make more or less than five, and so forth; all of which I see clearly cannot be otherwise than I conceive it to be.

Besides, since I have no reason to believe in the existence of such a deceiving Being, nor so far in the existence of any God at all, my reason for doubting, as it hangs on a mere conjecture, is but a slender and, so to speak, metaphysical reason. Nevertheless, this doubt too should be raised, and, in order to do so, I must consider at the first opportunity whether God exists, and, if He does, whether He can be a deceiver, for without assurance on these two points I do not see how it is possible to be certain of anything. In order, however, that I may have the opportunity of examining these two questions without interrupting the order of these Meditations, which is to begin with the first notions I find in my mind and to proceed step by step to the later ones, I must at this point classify all my ideas and decide in which classes truth and error are properly to be found.

Among these ideas are those which resemble images, and it is to them that the term *idea* properly belongs; as for instance the idea of a man, or of a monster, of heaven, of an angel, or of God Himself. In other cases, I conceive in another way, as when I will or fear, affirm or deny, for then I conceive something to be the matter of my thought, but the action of my mind adds something to the representation; and here we have conations and affections of the mind, on the one hand, and judgements on the other.

Now, as to the ideas taken in themselves, without reference to anything else, they are, properly speaking, never false; for, whether I imagine a goat or a ghoul, it is as true that I imagine the one as the other. Nor is there any fear of falsehood in the will or the affections; for, though what I desire may be bad, or even non-existent, it remains true that I desire it. Thus there remain only the judgements, in which I must take great care not to be mistaken; and here the principal and most common mistake I can make is to judge that the ideas inside my mind resemble things outside my mind, or are modelled upon them. Assuredly, if I looked upon my ideas simply as modes of my thought, without referring them to anything else, they could hardly afford me any occasion for error.

Ideas seem to be of three kinds – innate, adventitious, and fictitious: those that are born in me; those that come into my mind from outside, like strangers; and those I have made up and invented myself. The fact that I understand what is meant by a thing, or by a truth, or by a thought, all this seems to have no other origin than my own nature; while if now I hear a noise, if I see the sun, or if I feel heat, these sensations I have hitherto assumed to proceed from things outside myself; and, finally, sirens and griffins, and all such monsters, are the fictions and inventions of my mind. On the other hand I might perhaps make no distinctions and put all ideas together as having all entered my mind from outside, or as all born in me, or as all invented by me, for so far I have not perceived their origin clearly, and my chief task now is to consider those ideas which seem to emanate from things outside my mind, and to see on what grounds I regard them as modelled on those things.

Now, in the first place, this seems to be the teaching of nature; in the second, my experience tells me that these ideas do not depend upon my will, for they often come upon me despite myself, just as at the moment I feel heat, whether I want to or not, and this sensation, or this idea of heat appears to be produced in me by something other than myself, namely by the heat of the fire in front of which I am seated. Nothing seems more reasonable than to conclude that it is its own image, rather than something else, that the external thing impresses upon me.

But let me see if these arguments have sufficient force to convince me. When I speak of the teaching of nature, I mean by the expression only a certain impulse to believe, not some natural light in which my mind sees the truth; and between this impulse and this light there is a great disparity. What the natural light of my mind shows me to be true, that I cannot doubt, as it showed me a little while ago when from my doubt itself I was able to deduce my existence. Nor is there in my mind any other faculty, or power of distinguishing between the true and the false, in which I can place my trust to the same degree and which can prove to me that what the natural light of the mind shows to be true is in fact false. As to my natural impulses, I have often observed that they urge me towards the bad when it is a question of choosing the good, and I see no reason for trusting to them when it is a question of distinguishing between the true and the false.

Again, although the ideas we have been considering are independent of my will, it does not follow that they are produced necessarily by external things. Just as those impulses of which I spoke just now reside in me, although they are not always in agreement with my will, so there may be some faculty or power in me, of which I am still largely ignorant, capable of producing these ideas without any help from external things; and indeed, in sleep, such ideas seem to shape themselves in my mind without any assistance from the things they represent. Finally, even if it were true that these ideas came from things that are different from me, it does not follow that they resemble them; on the contrary, I have often observed a great difference between the representation and what it is supposed to represent. For example, I find in my mind two quite different ideas of the sun. One is drawn from the senses and must be placed in the category of ideas I have called adventitious; it makes the sun appear extremely small. The other is based upon the arguments of Astronomy, and is drawn, that is to say, from ideas born in me, or made up by me in some way or other; it shows the sun as several times larger than the earth. The two ideas cannot both be a likeness of the sun, and reason persuades me that it is the first idea, which seems to follow immediately upon the appearance, which is particularly unlike the original.

All this shows clearly enough that hitherto my belief in the existence of things outside me which impress their ideas or images on my mind by means of the senses, or in some other way, has been founded not on a sure judgement, but on a blind impulse.

There is, however, still another way of enquiring whether among the ideas that inhabit my mind some represent things outside it. So long as these ideas are considered simply as certain ways of thinking I can discern no difference or inequality among them, and all seem to proceed from me in the same way; but, if I regard them as representations, one representing one thing, and one another, then it is obvious that they differ greatly among themselves. Those that represent substances are without doubt something more, and have more reality, so to speak, as objects in the mind, than those which represent modes or accidents. Moreover, the idea by which I conceive of a sovereign, eternal, and infinite God, omniscient and omnipotent, the universal Creator of all things that exist outside Him – such an idea, I say, must have in itself more reality than those which represent finite substances to me.

Now it is something manifest to the natural light of the mind that there must be at least as much reality in the efficient and total cause as in its effect. For whence does the effect draw its reality except from the cause? And how can the cause communicate this reality, unless it has it in itself?

From this it follows that nothingness can produce nothing, and that the more perfect, or more real, cannot follow and depend upon the less perfect. And this truth is evident and clear not only in the case of effects possessing what the Schoolmen[1] call an actual or formal reality,[2] but also in the case of ideas in which the reality considered is only objective,[2] that is to say, representational. Not only can a stone, which has never existed, not begin to exist unless it is produced by something which possesses, either formally or virtually, all that is found in the stone, which contains, that is to say, all the properties, or other more excellent ones, that exist in the stone; and not only can heat not be produced in a subject except by something of an order at least as perfect as that of heat; but the idea of the stone, or of heat, cannot exist in me unless it has been put into my mind by a cause in which I conceive as much reality as in the heat or the stone. For, although this cause transmits nothing of its actual or formal reality to the idea, it is not to be thought that this cause should be less real than the idea. What must be realized is that every idea being a product of the mind requires of itself no more formal reality than it receives or borrows from

1. The Scholastics.
2. See Note on Cartesian Terminology, p. 192.

thought, or the mind, of which it is simply a mode, that is to say, a manner or way of thinking. Now for an idea to contain this particular objective reality rather than another it must without doubt receive it from some cause which contains at least as much of formal reality as the idea contains of objective reality, that is, of reality as an object in the mind. For, if we suppose that the idea contains something that is not found in its cause, then this extra something must come from nothing. Besides, however imperfect this mode of being may be, by which a thing exists objectively in the understanding through its idea, it cannot be nothing, nor can it come from nothing. For, just as this manner of objective being belongs to ideas by their very nature, so formal being belongs by their nature to the causes of these ideas, or at least to the first and principal of these causes. And, though one idea can give birth to another, there cannot be an infinite regression, but one must in the end reach the first idea of which the cause is, as it were, a type or pattern containing as much formal reality, or perfection,[1] as there is objective, or representational, reality in the idea. Thus the natural light of the mind shows me with evidence that ideas are in me like pictures or images, which can indeed fall short of the perfections of the things from which they derive, but which can never contain anything greater or more perfect.

Now, the longer and the more minutely I examine all this, the more clearly and distinctly do I know it all to be true. What conclusion, then, shall I come to? That the objective reality of some of my ideas is such that I know clearly that it does not exist in me formally or virtually, and that consequently I cannot myself be its cause. It follows necessarily that I am not alone in the world, but that something else exists; whereas, if there were no idea of the kind to be found in me, I should have no argument

1. See Note on Cartesian Terminology, p. 191.

to convince me and make me certain of the existence of anything other than myself; for I have examined all these arguments carefully and found them all wanting.

Among my ideas, in addition to the one which represents me to myself about which there can be no difficulty here, there is one which represents God, others which represent physical and inanimate things, others which represent angels and animals, and others, finally, which represent men similar to myself. As to the ideas which represent other men, or animals, or angels, I easily conceive that I can compose them of the ideas I have of myself, of physical things, and of God, even if, outside myself, there existed in the world no men, no animals, and no angels. As to the ideas of physical things, there is nothing in them which, as it seems, I could not produce myself; for, if I look at them more closely, and examine them as I examined the idea of wax yesterday, I find very little I can perceive distinctly and clearly beyond their magnitude or extension in length, breadth, and depth, figures which result from the limits of extension, the position which bodies of different figure preserve among themselves, and movement or change of position; to which may be added substance, duration, and number. But as for the rest, such as light, colour, sound, smell, taste, heat, cold, and the qualities which belong to touch, they appear with such obscurity and confusion in my mind that I do not even know whether they are true or false – whether, that is to say, the ideas I have of them represent real things or nothing. For, although I have previously observed that only a judgement can properly be called false, there is a certain material falsity in ideas when they represent as real something that does not exist. Thus, for example, the ideas I have of heat and cold are so far from clear and distinct that it is impossible to learn from them whether cold is an absence of heat, or heat an absence of cold, whether either is a real quality, or neither. Now as ideas, being like images, must seem to be the ideas of things, if it be indeed true that cold is nothing but the absence of heat, the idea which represents it to me as something real and definite is not undeservedly called false; and the same may be said of other similar ideas, to which I need ascribe no other author than myself. If they are false, if, that is to say, they represent nothing, the natural light of my mind shows me that they come from nothing, and the fact that I have them points to some deficiency and imperfection in myself. If they are true, they exhibit so little reality that I cannot distinguish them from nothingness, and I do not see why they should not have been produced by me.

As for the clear and distinct ideas I have about physical things, there are some, it seems, I may have been able to derive from the idea I have of myself, namely the ideas of substance, of duration, and of number, and other similar ideas, if there be any such. When I think of a stone, for instance, as a substance, that is, as a thing capable of subsisting of itself, since I am myself a substance, and although I am a thinking not an extended thing, and a stone is an extended not a thinking thing, so that there is a notable difference between the two conceptions, nevertheless they have this point in common that both represent substances. In the same way, when I observe that I exist now, and recollect that I existed in the past, and when I conceive various thoughts, of which I know the number, my mind acquires the ideas of duration and number, which I can thereafter apply to anything I please.

With regard, now, to those properties of which the ideas of physical things are composed, namely extension, shape, position, and movement, it is true that they cannot exist formally in me, since I am merely a thinking thing, but because they are the modes of substance, the garments, as it were, in which substance is clad, and because I am myself a substance, it seems that they might be contained in me virtually.

Thus there remains only the idea I have of God in which I may consider whether there is anything which could not have come from me. By the word God I mean an infinite, eternal, immutable, and independent substance, all-knowing and all-powerful, cause and creator of myself and of anything else whatsoever that may exist. And these attributes are of such a nature that the more attentively I contemplate them, the less it seems that the whole conception can come from me. The necessary conclusion, which follows from all that I have already said, is that God exists; for, although the idea of substance is in me by the very fact that I am myself a substance, I should not have the idea of an infinite substance, since I am myself a finite being, if it had not been placed in me by a substance that was truly infinite.

Nor am I to imagine that my idea of the infinite[1] is not a true one, and that I conceive it by negation of the finite: just as I conceive rest and darkness by the negation of movement and light. On the contrary, I see clearly that there is more reality in an infinite substance than in a finite substance, and thus that the whole notion of the infinite is, in a sense, anterior in me to the notion of the finite, that the idea of God is anterior, that is to say, to the idea of myself; for how would it be possible for me to know that I doubt, or that I desire, that is, that I am wanting in something and am not all perfect, if there were no idea in my mind of a being more perfect than myself by comparison with which I know the deficiencies of my own nature.

And it cannot be said that this idea of God is materially false, and that I can derive it consequently from nothing, that is to say, that I have the idea because of some imperfection in me, as I said just now of the ideas of cold

1. See Note on Cartesian Terminology, p. 191.

and heat, and other similar ideas. On the contrary, as the idea of God is particularly clear and distinct, and contains in itself more objective reality than any other, there is none that is more true in itself, and less open to the suspicion that it is false. This idea, I say, of a sovereignly perfect and infinite being is wholly true. A pretence can be made that no such being exists; there can be no pretence that its idea represents nothing real to me, as I have said was the case with the idea of cold. And the idea of God, being particularly clear and distinct, contains wholly within itself all that I perceive to be real and true and as having some degree of perfection. Nor is it any objection that I cannot comprehend the infinite, or that there are in God an infinity of properties that my mind cannot embrace, and which are quite outside the range of my thoughts, for it is of the nature of the infinite that it should surpass my own nature which is finite and limited; and it is enough for me to understand and judge that everything I perceive clearly and know to have some degree of perfection or reality, as well perhaps as a host of other things I am ignorant of, exists either formally or virtually in God for the idea I have of God to be at once the truest, the clearest, and the most distinct, of all the ideas I have in my mind.

But perhaps – it may be argued – perhaps I am something greater than I take myself to be; perhaps all these perfections I attribute to the nature of a God, are in me potentially, even though they have not yet been realized or shown themselves in act. For my experience teaches me that my knowledge increases and grows more perfect little by little, and I see no reason why it should not grow to infinity and, being thus augmented and made perfect, acquire for me all the remaining perfections that belong to the Divine nature; and if I have this power, the power to acquire these attributes, that should be sufficient for my own mind to produce the ideas of them.

Of course, there is nothing in all this. In the first place, true though it is that my knowledge increases by degrees and that I have many potentialities which have not yet been actualized, these facts have no relation to my idea of God from which potentiality is entirely absent, and the fact that my knowledge grows greater little by little is a certain argument for its imperfection. Besides, even if my knowledge increases gradually, I know well enough that it will never be infinite in act, that it will never reach such a pitch of perfection as to be incapable of further growth. But God I judge to be infinite in act so that nothing can be added to the sovereign perfection He possesses. Finally, I see that the objective being of an idea cannot be caused by a potential being, which is properly speaking nothing, but only by an actual or formal being.

Now, in all that I have just said, there is nothing, certainly, that is not manifest in the natural light of the mind to anyone who considers the matter attentively. I find, however, when I relax my attention, that my mind being darkened and, as it were, blinded by the images of physical things no longer finds it easy to recall the reason why the idea I have of a being more perfect than myself must necessarily have been caused in me by such a being. That is why I wish to take a further step and to ask whether, having this idea of God, I could still exist if no God existed.

And, in that case, if there were no God, whence should I derive my existence? From myself, perhaps, or from my parents, or from causes less perfect than God than whom nothing can be conceived or imagined more perfect.

But if I existed of myself, as the author of my own being, I should have no doubts of anything, I should harbour no desires, I should be wanting in nothing; I should have bestowed upon myself all the perfections of which I had any idea, and thus I should be God. Nor am I to imagine it more difficult to acquire other perfections than those I possess. On the contrary, it was clearly far more difficult for me, a thinking thing or substance, to emerge out of nothingness than merely to add to the accidents[1] of that substance by acquiring the knowledge of many things I did not know. Thus if all this further knowledge had come to me of myself, that is to say, if I were the author of my own being, I should certainly not have deprived myself of what is easier to acquire, nor indeed of any of those other attributes which I see to be contained in my idea of God. Nothing, in truth, seems to me more difficult than the accomplishment of my own existence, and, if there were, I should soon recognize it as such (always supposing that everything else I possess, I possess of myself), and as the point at which my power ended.

Nor do I escape the force of these arguments by supposing that I have always existed, as I exist now, as if it followed that there was no need, consequently, to seek the author of my existence. For the whole duration of my life can be divided into an infinity of parts, all independent of each other, and so from the fact that I have already existed it does not follow that I should exist now, unless there were some cause to create me again at each moment, and preserve me in existence. To anyone attentively considering the nature of time it is quite obvious that for a substance to be preserved through every moment of its duration the same force and action are required as to create it again from nothing. Thus the natural light of the mind shows that the distinction we make between creation and preservation in time is a distinction in thought only, and not in fact.

The next step I should take, then, is to ask myself if I have the power to ensure that I, who exist at this moment, shall do so in the immediate future. Now, as I am a thinking thing, or as that is the only part of me I am at present considering, if I had any such power, I should

1. Acquired qualities.

without any doubt whatever be conscious of it; but, on the contrary, I have no such thought, and I am thereby aware that I depend upon some being other than myself.

Perhaps, however, this being, on whom I depend, is not what I call God, perhaps I owe my being to my parents, or to some cause less perfect than God. Far from it; as I have already said, it is obvious that there must be as much reality in the cause as in the effect, and as I am a thinking thing, having an idea of God, whatever be the cause attributed to my being, it must itself be a thinking thing, and possess in itself the idea of all the perfections I attribute to the Divine nature. Next, one may enquire if this cause exists of itself, or is dependent on some other being, for, if it exists of itself, it follows from what I have said that it is God, because, as it has the power of existing of itself, so it must have the power of possessing in act all the perfections of which it has the idea, all the perfections, that is to say, I conceive of as existing in God. But if it derives its existence from some other being, then we may enquire if this second cause exists of itself, or through another, until step by step we reach the last cause, which will be God. And it is manifest enough that there can be no infinite regress in this case, for we are concerned, not so much with the origin of my being, as with what sustains it at each moment of time.

Nor can there be any pretence that a number of partial causes have contributed to give me existence, and that from one I have acquired the idea of one of the perfections of God, and from another the idea of another, so that it may be said that, although all these perfections exist somewhere in the universe, they do not all meet together in one Being, who is God. On the contrary, the unity, the simplicity or inseparability, of all the attributes I conceive of as belonging to Him is one of His principal perfections. And, certainly, the idea of this unity of all His perfections could not have been placed in my mind by any cause without the ideas of all these perfections, for I could not conceive of them as united and inseparable without knowing, in some sense, what they were.

As for my parents, even though all that I have ever thought of them be true, it cannot certainly be argued that they have caused and sustained my existence as a thinking thing, their function being limited to conditioning the matter in which my mind, which is all I at present take to be myself, is immersed. There can be no difficulty with regard to them; and we must necessarily conclude that from the fact that I exist and have in me the idea of a sovereignly perfect being, that is to say, of God, the existence of God is most evidently proved.

There only remains for me to enquire how I acquired this idea. I have not received it through the senses; it has never presented itself to me against my expectations, as happens with the ideas of physical things when they present themselves, or seem to present themselves, to the external organs of my senses. Nor is it an invention of my mind, for I can add nothing to it, nor diminish it. All that remains to be said, consequently, is that, like the idea of myself, it was placed in me at the moment of my creation.

Now, certainly, there is nothing strange about the fact that God, in creating me, should have placed this idea of Himself in me to serve, as it were, as the imprint of the workman upon his work. Nor is it necessary that the imprint should differ from the work itself. On the contrary, from the mere fact that God has created me, it becomes highly credible that He should have made me in His own image and resemblance, and that I should perceive this resemblance (in which the idea of God is contained) by means of the very faculty that enables me to perceive myself; that is to say, when I reflect upon myself, not only do I know myself as an imperfect being, incomplete and dependent on some other being, aspiring endlessly to something higher and better than myself, but I know at the same time that this being on whom I depend possesses all these high attributes to which I aspire and of which I have some idea, not by way of tendency or potentiality merely, but actually and to an infinite degree, and that thus this being is God. The whole force of the argument I have used in proving the existence of God resides in this, that I understand that my nature could not be what it is, that I could not have in me, that is to say, the idea of a God, if God did not truly exist, that same God whose idea inhabits me, who possesses all those perfections of which I can have some idea without, indeed, being able to comprehend them altogether, and who is subject to no defects. It follows that God does not deceive us, for deceit is the sign of a defect.

But, now, before I scrutinize all this more closely, and turn to the consideration of those other truths which may be derived from it, it seems to me fitting that I should pause for a time in the contemplation of this God, that I should ponder all His attributes, consider, admire, and adore the incomparable beauty of this immeasurable light, at least as much as my mind, dazzled by so much splendour, has the power to do. For, as in the next life the contemplation of the Divine Majesty, as our faith teaches, will be our supreme happiness, so even now we can learn from experience how a meditation of this kind, though incomparably less perfect, affords us the greatest joy we are capable of feeling in this life.

4

OF TRUTH AND FALSEHOOD

[But if God does not deceive me, and has given me my intelligence, how is error possible? Or is God responsible for my faults? The answer lies in the fact that the capacity of my will far exceeds the capacity of my finite intelligence; indeed it is in my will, with its seemingly limitless scope, that I most resemble the infinity or God. Now it is through the will that I affirm something to be true or good, and the tendency of my will is to carry me beyond what I perceive clearly and distinctly, and so to make me fall into error or sin. The remedy is steadfastly to remember the necessity of basing my judgements on what my mind perceives clearly and distinctly. Thus will I avoid error and attain to the truth in all things.]

I HAVE so accustomed myself these last few days to detaching my mind from the senses, and have become so well aware how little we know with certainty about physical things, and how much more we know about the mind, and even about God Himself, that it is now very easy for me to turn away my thoughts from what belongs to the senses and to the imagination, and to fix them on what, being free of matter, is purely intelligible.

Certainly, the idea I have of the human mind insofar as it is a thinking thing, without extension in length, breadth, and depth, and having nothing that pertains to bodies, is incomparably more distinct than the idea of any physical thing. And when I reflect that I doubt, that is to say, that I am an incomplete and dependent being, the idea of a complete and independent being, the idea, that is, of God, presents itself with unrivalled distinction and clarity to my mind; and, from the mere fact that such an idea should be in me, or that I, who have this idea, exist, I am so convinced both that God exists and that my existence depends upon Him at every moment of my life that I do not think there is anything the human mind can know with greater evidence and certainty. Already, then, I think I have discovered the road which will lead us from the contemplation of the true God (in whom are enclosed all the treasures of knowledge and wisdom) to the knowledge of everything else.

In the first place, I recognize that it is impossible that God should ever deceive me, since deceit is an imperfection, and, although the ability to deceive may seem a sign of subtlety or power, there is no doubt that the will to deceive is evidence of either weakness or malice. Nothing of this is to be found in God.

Secondly, I am aware in myself of a certain power of judgement, and, like all my other powers, it must be bestowed upon me by God; moreover, as He does not wish to deceive me, this power cannot be of such a kind as to lead me into error when I make a proper use of it. Nor would any doubt be left of this truth, did it not seem to imply that I can, in consequence, never be mistaken; for, if everything I have comes from God, and if He has bestowed upon me no power to go astray, it does not seem as if I could ever be at fault. And, indeed, when I think only of God, and turn myself wholly towards Him, I can find in myself no cause of error or falsehood. Soon after, however, when I come back to myself, I discover a countless host of errors, and, when I enquire further as to their cause, I observe that my mind contains not only a real and positive idea of God, the idea of a sovereign and perfect being, but a pure negation, the idea of nothingness,[1] or of that which is infinitely removed from all perfection. Thus do I remain poised between God and nothingness, between the fullness of being and its absence, so that, as I have been created by the Supreme Being, there is nothing in me to make me fall into error, but, as there is in me some element of nothingness or non-being, as I am not, in fact, the Supreme Being, so am

1. See Note on Cartesian Terminology, p. 192.

I the subject of innumerable deficiencies, and it is no wonder when I go wrong. Hence the conclusion I can draw with certainty that error is nothing real and so dependent on God, but simply a defect or deficiency, and I can go wrong, not because God has bestowed upon me a special faculty for falling into error, but because my power of judging truly, which He has given me, is not an infinite power.

This conclusion, however, is not completely satisfactory, for error is not a pure negation, it is not, that is to say, the mere want of some perfection which is my due, but rather the privation or lack of some knowledge which I ought, apparently, to possess. If we consider the nature of God, it seems impossible to me that He should have granted me a faculty which is imperfect in its kind, which is lacking, that is to say, in the perfection which is its due. The more highly skilled the artisan, the more perfect, the more accomplished, the work of his hands. Can we imagine the Creator of all things as producing some being incomplete in anything that its nature requires? There is no doubt that God could have created me such as to be incapable of error; nor is there any doubt that He always desires the best. Now which is better – that I should err sometimes, or always?

Meanwhile, as I ponder all this more attentively, the first thought that occurs to me is that it is not to be wondered at if my intelligence is incapable of grasping why God does what He does, and that I have consequently no reason to doubt His existence because my experience may show me many other things without my being able to understand why or how God has created them. Knowing already that my nature is extremely weak and limited, while the nature of God is, on the contrary, immeasurable, incomprehensible, and infinite, I have no further trouble in recognizing that there lie within His power infinite possibilities of which the causes are beyond the scope of my mind; and this is enough by itself to show that what are called final causes are of no use at all in Natural Philosophy, nor is it without temerity that it would be possible for me to undertake to probe the impenetrable purposes of God.

The next thought that came to my mind was that whenever we enquire into the perfection of the works of God, we should consider the universe with all it contains as a whole, not each creature separately; for the same being which, taken by itself, appears with some reason to be highly imperfect, reveals, when taken as a part of the whole universe, the full perfection of its nature. For my part, although I have undertaken to doubt all things, and am certain only of my own existence and God's, now that I have recognized His infinite power, 1 cannot deny that He may have created, or could create, a host of beings among whom I have my place as part of the universe.

Finally, when I scrutinize myself more closely, and take account of the errors I commit (errors which are the only mark of imperfection in me), I see that they depend upon the conjunction of two causes, upon the power I have of knowing things, and upon the power I have of choosing between them which is my free-will; they depend, that is to say, at the same time upon my understanding and upon my will. By my understanding alone I neither affirm nor deny anything, I merely perceive the ideas I can affirm or deny. In this precise sense, it may be said that there is never any error in the understanding, provided the word error is taken in its proper signification. And although there may be an infinity of things in the world of which I have no idea in my mind, it cannot be said that my mind has been deprived of this knowledge as of something which is its due, but simply as something my mind is without, since there is, in fact, nothing to suggest that God should have given me a more ample power of knowing than I have received from Him, and, skilled artisan though I conceive Him to be, I am not on that account to consider that He should put into each one of His works as much perfection as He can in some. Nor can I complain that He has made my free-will less absolute, less far-ranging, than it should be; for I feel it to be without limits. And what seems particularly to be remarked here is that there is not one of my other faculties but I conceive that it could be more perfect and of greater scope. If, for example, I consider my power of understanding, I know at once how exiguous and limited it is, and at the same time I have the idea of another similar faculty much wider in scope and even infinite – which idea, from the mere fact that I have it, makes me see that such a faculty pertains to the nature of God. In the same way, if I examine my memory, or my imagination, or some other faculty, I find I have none that is not feeble and limited, whereas in God the same faculty is unlimited and infinite. It is only the power of my will which I feel to be so great that I cannot form the idea of anything of greater scope, so that it is chiefly through my will that I bear the image and resemblance of God. For, even though the will of God is incomparably greater than mine because of the power and knowledge which are joined with it and render it firmer and more efficacious, or because of its object which extends so much more widely, yet in itself, taken precisely and formally, it does not seem greater. In what does the power of the will consist? In being able to do, or not to do, something – in affirming or denying it, pursuing or avoiding it; or perhaps rather in affirming or denying, pursuing or avoiding, what the intelligence proposes for our consideration, without feeling that our choice is imposed upon us by some external power. Nor is it necessary, in order to be free, that I should be quite indifferent as between two opposing tendencies. On the contrary, the more I incline towards one side rather than the other, either because I see it to contain the true and the good, or because God has so disposed my mind from within, the more freely do I choose, since neither the grace of God, assuredly, nor the natural working of my intelligence, can in any way diminish my freedom; rather do they increase and fortify it. The indifference I feel, when there is no reason why I should incline to one side or the other, is thus the lowest degree of freedom, and displays rather a defect of know-ledge than the perfection of the will; for, if I always knew clearly what is true and what is good, I should never be at pains to deliberate over my judgement or my choice, and thus I should be entirely free without ever being indifferent.

From all this I perceive that it is neither the power of the will, which I have received from God, which is in itself the cause of my errors (for its scope is of the widest and it is perfect in its kind), nor the power of knowing, for whatever I know, I know because God has given me the power of knowing, and in that I cannot err. Whence, then, do my errors arise? From this one fact that, as my will is much wider in scope than my understanding, I cannot contain the former within the limits of the latter, but extend it to what goes beyond my grasp, and here the will, being indifferent of itself, easily goes astray, choosing the bad instead of the good, and the false in-stead of the true. Thus is it that I fall into error, or com-mit sins.

For example, when a few days ago I was enquiring as to whether anything at all existed in the world, and con-cluded that from the fact that I was myself considering the question, it followed evidently that I existed, I could not avoid judging that what I understood so clearly was true, not because I was forced to the conclusion by some external force, but simply because the great clarity of my perception was followed by a strong inclination of my will, and my conclusion was all the more free as it was less indifferent. On the other hand, I know at the moment no more than that I exist as a thinking thing, but I also have a certain idea of physical nature which makes me doubt whether my thinking nature, the nature which makes me what I am, is different from physical nature, or whether both natures are not identical. And suppose there is no reason to make me incline to one conclusion or the other, it follows that I am entirely indifferent as to which I deny or affirm, or even as to whether I suspend my judgement.

And this indifference extends not only to cases where the understanding has no knowledge, but generally also to those where there is a lack of perfect clarity at the moment when the will is engaged in deliberation. But however probable may be the conjectures which influence my judgement in particular cases, the mere fact that they are conjectures, and not certain and indubitable arguments, is enough to make the contrary judgement possible. I myself have had sufficient experience of this during the past few days when I posited as false all that I had hitherto taken to be true simply because I had observed that doubt was possible.

Now, if I abstain from making a judgement about something which I do not perceive clearly and distinctly enough, I do well, and I do not fall into error; but if I risk an assurance or a denial, then I do not make a right use of my free-will, and if I assert what is false, then am I plainly at fault; while even if my assertion turns out to be true, that is but the effect of chance, and I am still at fault in myself, and still misusing my free-will. For the natural light of the mind makes it manifest that perception by the understanding should always precede the determination of the will. And it is in this misuse of my free-will that the defect resides which is the formal constituent of error — a defect, I say, which belongs to the operation insofar as it depends on me, not to the faculty

I have received from God, nor to the operation as it depends upon Him.

I have no reason, further, to complain that God has not given me a greater power of understanding, or a greater natural light of the mind, for it is of the nature of the human understanding that it should not understand many things, as it is of the nature of the created intellect that it should be finite; but I have every reason to render Him thanks for what He has bestowed upon me, when nothing is my due, and without supposing that I have been unjustly deprived of what He has not given me.

Then, as to my will ranging more widely than my understanding, here too I have no grounds for complaint, since the will, being by nature one and indivisible, can hardly be limited without its nature being destroyed. Indeed, the wider its scope, the more should I render thanks to the Giver.

Finally, I have no right to complain because I remain dependent upon the power of God for the formation of those acts of the will or of judgement which lead me into error. The acts themselves are altogether good and true insofar as they depend upon God, and there is, in a sense, greater perfection in my nature because I can form them than if I could not. As for the defect, or deficiency, which is the formal constituent of error and of sin, this is nothing real and does not depend upon God as something that exists, so that its relation to God is not that of a positive privation, as the Schoolmen call it, but of a mere negation or absence. Assuredly, it is no imperfection in God that He should have endowed me with the freedom to give or to withhold my assent in cases where He has not endowed my understanding with a clear and distinct perception of the facts. The imperfection is without doubt in me for misusing my liberty, and proffering my judgement on what I perceive only obscurely and confusedly.

Of course I see, nevertheless, that it would have been easy for God so to arrange matters that I should never err, despite my freedom and my limited power of knowing, either by giving my understanding a clear and distinct perception of everything on which I should have to deliberate, or by engraving so deeply on my memory the resolution never to form a judgement without this clear and distinct perception that I should never forget it. And I easily understand that, if I consider only myself, as if I were alone in the universe, I should be much more perfect than I am, if God had made me in such a way as to be faultless. What I cannot deny is that there is in a sense greater perfection in the universe, if some of its parts are subject to defect, while others are not, than if all are entirely alike. As for myself, I have no right to complain if God has not called upon me to play the leading and most perfect rôle in the whole universe. Besides, although God has not granted me the first means of remaining free from error, which consists in always enjoying a clear and evident knowledge of whatever I need to consider, He has left the other means in my power, which is to remember never to give my judgement in cases where the truth is not clearly known to me. For, although I know my own weakness which makes it impossible for me to fix my mind at all times on a single thought, yet by careful and constant meditation on the point I can so imprint it on my memory as never to forget it each time I need it, and so I may acquire the habit of never going astray. Finally, since it is in this respect, in the knowledge of the truth, that the true greatness and perfection of man consists, I consider that I have gained more than a little from this Meditation in having discovered the cause of falsehood and error.

Certainly, there can be no other cause than the one I have set forth. As often as I so contain my will within the limits of the understanding that it is only concerned with what appears clearly and distinctly in the light of the mind, then I can never go wrong. Every clear and distinct perception is something real and positive, and must therefore proceed, not from nothing, but from God – from God, I say, who, being the Supreme Perfection, can never be the source of error; and thus such a perception, such a judgement, is indubitably true. Besides, what I have learned in this Meditation, is not simply how to avoid error, but how to reach the truth. For I shall reach it, if only I am sufficiently attentive to whatever I perceive clearly and distinctly, and separate these perceptions clearly from what I apprehend obscurely and confusedly. Such is the task to which I must henceforth devote myself.

5

OF THE ESSENCE OF MATERIAL THINGS, AND THEREBY OF GOD, THAT HE EXISTS

[*So far I know only that God exists and that I exist. Does anything else exist? I consider the objects of mathematical knowledge, and immediately I come upon a second proof of the existence of God. If I have the idea of a triangle in my mind, I do not know whether it exists or not outside my mind; but if I have, as I certainly have, the idea of God, I see at once that the idea of God involves the existence of God. For just as the idea of a triangle involves all the essential properties of a triangle as that its three angles are equal to two right angles, so the idea of God involves existence as one of the essential properties, or attributes, of God. I perceive this clearly and distinctly. What can be meant by a non-existent God? And I know, too, that all certitude in the sciences depends upon Him.*]

I STILL have a number of questions to consider regarding the attributes of God and the properties of my own nature, that is to say, of the nature of my mind; but I shall return to them, perhaps, at some other time. For the moment, having observed what must be done, or avoided, in order to reach the knowledge of the truth, my chief task is to rid myself of all those doubts with which I have been encumbered these past few days, and to see if anything certain can be known about material things.

I must, however, before asking whether such things exist outside me, examine the ideas I have of them so as to distinguish between those that are distinct and those that are confused.

Now, in the first place, I have a distinct image of that quantity which philosophers commonly call continuous quantity, the extension, that is to say, in length, breadth, and depth, of that quantity, or rather of the thing to which quantity is attributed. In addition, I can count its several parts, attributing to each various sizes, figures, locations, and movements; and, finally, I can assign duration, in varying degrees, to these movements.

And all this I know not only distinctly, when I consider it in general, but I have only to apply my attention to become aware of a host of particulars regarding numbers, figures, movements, and so on, of which the truth appears with so much evidence, and seems so connatural with my mind, that it does not seem so much that I am learning something new as that I am recalling what I knew before, or perceiving what I already had in my mind, although I had not yet turned my thoughts in that direction.

But what I find most worthy of consideration here is that I find I have a multitude of ideas of various things that cannot be regarded as nothing, although they may have no existence outside my mind, and which are not invented by me, even though I am free to conceive them or not, as I please, and which, finally, possess their own true and unalterable nature. When, for example, I imagine a triangle, although perhaps there is not, and never has been, any place in which it can exist outside my mind, yet this triangle possesses a nature, or form, or essence, which is immutable and eternal, which I have not invented, and which in no way depends upon my mind. This follows from the fact that it is possible to demonstrate various properties of the triangle, as that its three angles are equal to two right angles, that the largest angle is subtended by the longest side, and so on, all of which, whether I wish to or not, I recognize to be very clearly and evidently contained in it, even though, when I first imagined a triangle, I had no thought of these properties, which cannot therefore have been invented by me.

Nor can I make the objection that perhaps the idea of a triangle reached me through my senses, because I have sometimes seen bodies that are triangular in shape. The fact is that I can conceive a mass of other figures, about which there can never be any suspicion that they have come under the observation of my senses, but of which I can demonstrate various properties touching their essence as I can in the case of the triangle. Now, these properties, as I conceive them clearly, must all be true, and therefore something, not nothing; for it is evident that what is true is real, and I have already proved that whatever I know clearly and distinctly is true. Besides, even though I have not demonstrated it, the nature of my mind is such that as long as I perceive something clearly and distinctly I must regard it as true. I remember, too, that while I was still in bondage to my senses I counted among the most certain and evident truths those that pertained to number and figure and to everything else that is part of arithmetic or geometry.

And now, if from the fact that I can form the idea of a thing in my mind it follows that whatever I recognize clearly and distinctly as belonging to that thing, belongs to it in fact, can I not argue in the same way to a demonstrative proof of the existence of God? It is certain that I have the idea of God, the idea of a sovereignly perfect Being, in my mind no less than the idea of some figure or number. I know no less clearly and distinctly that eternal existence belongs to the nature of God than I know that certain properties I demonstrate of some number or figure belong to the nature of that number or figure. Indeed, even if everything I have said in the preceding Meditations were shown not to be true, I should at least regard the existence of God as being at least as certain as the truths I have accepted of mathematics.

This assertion, it is true, may not seem manifest at first, and may even take on the appearance of a sophism. I am accustomed with everything else to make a distinction between existence and essence, and so I easily persuade myself that God's existence can be separated from His essence, and that I can think of Him as not actually existing. However, if I consider the matter more carefully, it becomes manifest that existence can no more be separated from the essence of God than the fact that the three angles of a triangle are together equal to two right angles can be separated from it, or again, than the idea of a mountain can be separated from the idea of a valley. Thus there is no less contradiction in the conception of a God (that is to say, of a sovereignly perfect Being) who lacks existence (that is to say, who lacks a particular perfection) than in the conception of a mountain without a valley.

It may be objected that, though it is true that God cannot be thought of as non-existent any more than a mountain can be conceived without a valley, from the fact that I conceive a mountain with a valley it does not follow that there is any mountain; in the same way, although I conceive God as existing, it does not follow that God exists, since my thought imposes no necessity on existence. I can well imagine a winged horse, though no such horse exists, and so perhaps I could attribute existence to God, though no God exists. But the argument is a fallacy, and a sophism lurks behind the objection I have put forward. From the fact that I cannot conceive a mountain without a valley, it does not follow that there is in the world any mountain, or any valley, but only that the mountain and the valley, whether they exist or not, cannot be separated from each other; but from the fact that I cannot conceive God except as existing, it follows that existence is inseparable from Him, and therefore that He exists in truth; not that my thought can make it so, and impose its own necessity on the facts, but, on the contrary, because the necessity of the fact itself, namely, the existence of God, determines my mind to think in this way. I am not free to conceive a God without existence, to conceive, that is to say, a sovereign and perfect Being as lacking in a sovereign perfection, as I am free to imagine a horse with or without wings.

Nor can it be argued here that of course I must admit the existence of God, once I have supposed Him endowed with all perfections, existence being one of them, but that the supposition is itself unnecessary, just as it is unnecessary for me to suppose that all four-sided figures can be inscribed in a circle; for, if I do, I shall be constrained to admit that a rhombus can be inscribed in a circle, and so put forward a false conclusion. But this argument fails. True, I may never reach the idea of God, but every time I come to think of a first and sovereign Being, and to draw the idea of such a Being from the treasure-house of my mind, it is necessary that I should attribute to Him every kind of perfection, even though I cannot enumerate them all, or apply my attention to each one in particular. And this necessity is enough to make me conclude, once I have recognized that existence is a perfection, that this first and sovereign Being truly exists, just as there is no compelling reason why I should imagine a triangle, but whenever I take into consideration a rectilinear figure composed of only three angles, I am bound to attribute to it those properties which lead to the conclusion that its three angles are not greater than two right angles, even though I may not be concerned with this conclusion in particular at the moment. But when I consider what figures may be inscribed in a circle, there is no necessity for me to think that they include all four-sided figures; on the contrary, I cannot even pretend that it is so, as long as I am unwilling to accept in thought what is not clear and distinct. Consequently there is a great difference between false suppositions such as this and the true ideas that are born in me, of which the first and principal one is the idea of God.

Indeed, I recognize in a variety of ways that the idea of

God is not one I have invented, which depends only on my thought, but that it is the representation of a true and immutable nature. First, I can think only of God to whose essence existence belongs of necessity. Then, it is impossible to conceive two or several Gods in the same way. And, supposing that there is One now who exists, I see clearly that He must have existed from all eternity, and must continue to exist eternally. Finally, I perceive many other attributes in God which I can neither augment nor diminish.

In any case, whatever the proof or argument employed, one must always come back to the same point, that it is only what I perceive clearly and distinctly that has the power to convince me fully. Among the things I perceive in this way, some are in truth obvious to everyone, while others become apparent only to a closer consideration and a more exact scrutiny; nevertheless these last, once they have been discovered, have the same degree of certitude as the latter. For example, although in a right-angled triangle it is not so easily perceived that the square on the base is equal to the sum of the squares on the other two sides as it is evident that the base subtends the greatest angle, yet once the former conclusion has been ascertained, both are equally accepted as true. As regards God, were my mind not clouded with prejudice, and encumbered with the images of physical things, there is nothing I should know sooner or more easily than He. For there is nothing clearer or more manifest than the existence of a Supreme Being, or God, to whose essence alone existence belongs. True, in order to perceive this truth clearly I had need of great application, but now I am not only as certain of it as of the most certain thing I know, but I see besides that upon this certainty the certainty of everything else depends, so that without it nothing would be perfectly known.

For, although my nature is such that, as soon as I

understand something very clearly and distinctly, I cannot but think it true, nevertheless, because my nature is also such that my mind cannot remain indefinitely attached to the same object, and that I often recall that I have judged something to be true when I no longer have in mind the reasons for my judgement, it may happen that at such a moment I should be faced with arguments which might easily make me change my opinion, if I did not know there was a God. Thus I should never have a true and certain knowledge of anything at all, but only vague and wayward opinions. For example, when I consider the nature of a triangle, my knowledge of geometry shows me with the greatest evidence that its three angles are equal to two right angles, nor is it possible for me not to believe it as long as my thought applies itself to the proof; but, once I have withdrawn my attention, even though I remember that I had clearly understood it, I may easily come to doubt the truth, if I were ignorant of God. For I could persuade myself that nature had made me in such a way as to allow me to go wrong even in what I believed I understood with the greatest evidence and certitude, especially when I remember how much I have taken to be true and certain which later reasons have forced me to regard as absolutely false.

But now that I have recognized the existence of God, understanding at the same time that everything depends on Him and that He does not deceive us, and, further, that whatever I perceive clearly and distinctly cannot fail to be true, even though I am no longer thinking of the reasons for my judgement, provided only that I recall that I have clearly and distinctly grasped the matter, then no contrary reasons can be adduced to make me doubt my conclusion, and thus my knowledge is true and certain. And this same knowledge extends to everything I remember to have proved at some other time, as with the truths of geometry and so on. For what objection can be brought against this statement? Will it be said that I am highly prone to error? But I already know that I cannot be mistaken in my judgements when I know the reasons clearly. Will it be said that, in the past, I have held many things to be true and certain which I have afterwards repudiated as false? But, in those cases, I perceived nothing clearly and distinctly, and, being ignorant of this criterion of truth and falsehood, I accepted as conclusive reasons which I found later to be less solid than I had imagined. What else can be put forward? Perhaps, that I am asleep (an objection I have myself already raised), or that the thoughts in my mind are no more true than the dreams we have in sleep? But, even in sleep, what presents itself with evidence to my mind is absolutely true. And thus I recognize very clearly that the certitude and truth of all knowledge depends upon the knowledge of God alone so that, before I knew Him, I knew nothing perfectly. Now, however, that I do know Him, I have the means of acquiring a clear and evident knowledge of a host of things, not only concerning Him, but concerning physical nature insofar as it may be made the object of mathematical enquiry and proof.

6

OF THE EXISTENCE OF MATERIAL THINGS AND OF THE REAL DISTINCTION BETWEEN THE BODY AND SOUL OF MAN

[*To return to the question of the existence of the external world. God can certainly have made it; but from the idea of it as something extended in length, breadth, and depth, nothing can be deduced as to its existence, as the existence of God can be deduced from the idea of God. There is a clear difference between the intelligence which can subsist of itself and the imagination which suggests dependence upon a body as highly probable. But probability is not proof, and I cannot rely upon this argument. On the other hand my knowledge of God has dispelled my universal scepticism, and when I recall my previous doubts, I realize that memory enables me to distinguish satisfactorily between my dreams and my waking moments, and that my sensations have a certain practical reality in teaching me what to avoid and what to seek after for what appears to be my bodily good, even though they do not represent external qualities – what makes me feel hot is not hot in itself – and so they make the mind aware of the body with which it is intimately united, and consequently of the external world. Of course God could produce these sensations in me directly, but that would be a deceit, contrary to His Nature. Consequently the external world, including my body, exists, and the illusions of the senses, even in sickness, can be explained by the natural order of things. Thus, as all my faculties alike testify to the existence of the external world, I can have no reason, given the veracity of God, to deny it. Of course, human beings are prone to error, but the everyday business of living often gives us no time to pander our judgements, and we must always remember the weakness of human nature.*]

ALL that remains for me to do now is to enquire into the existence of material things, and I know at least this much already, that they can exist insofar as they are the objects of geometrical demonstrations, since then I perceive them very clearly and distinctly. For there is no doubt that God has the power to produce all those things I am able to perceive distinctly, the only things which, in my judgement, He cannot produce being those I am unable to have a distinct perception of without contradiction. Besides, my power of imagination, which I know I make use of in the consideration of material things, is capable of convincing me of their existence; for when I consider carefully what the imagination is, I find that it is nothing but the application of the faculty of knowing to a body which is intimately present to it, and which consequently exists.

And to make this plain, let me first note the difference between the imagination and pure intellection. For example, when I imagine a triangle, I do not simply understand it to be a figure composed of three lines, but I see these three lines as present, as it were, by the power of my mind, and that is what I call imagining. Now if I wish to think of a chiliagon, I quite understand that it is a figure composed of a thousand sides, just as easily as I understand that a triangle is a figure composed of three sides only, but I cannot imagine the thousand sides of the chiliagon as I can imagine the three sides of a triangle, nor see them as present, so to speak, to the eyes of my mind. Thus, although in accordance with my habit of using my imagination, when I think of a material thing, I have some sort of confused image in my mind in thinking of a chiliagon, it is obvious that this image does not represent a chiliagon, since there would be no difference in it if I were thinking of a myriagon, or any other many-sided figure, and since the image is of no assistance in the discovery of those properties that differentiate a chiliagon from any other polygon. Again, if it is a question of a pentagon, I understand what the figure is, just as I do that of a chiliagon, without recourse to my imagination; but I can also imagine a pentagon by applying the power of my mind to its five sides as well as to the area contained by these sides. I know, then, clearly that I need a particular effort of the mind in order to imagine, which I do not need in order to understand; and this effort clearly shows the difference there is between the imagination and the pure understanding.

I observe, further, that this power of imagining which is in me, insofar as it differs from my power of understanding, is in no way necessary to my nature or essence, that is to say, to the essence of my mind; for, even if I were entirely lacking in the faculty of imagination, I should no doubt still be what I am now, and so I may conclude, as it seems, that my imagination depends upon something other than my mind. If, then, a body exists so closely united with the mind that the mind can turn its attention to it when it pleases, I can easily understand that it is in this way that it forms the images of material things. It follows that this activity of the mind differs from pure intellection in that, in intellection, the mind turns back, as it were, upon itself and contemplates some of its own ideas, whereas in imagining it turns towards the body and inspects some idea it has itself formed or which it has received from the senses. It is easy, I say, to conceive of the imagination operating in this way, if it be true that bodies exist; and since I can find no other way of explaining the imagination, I may conjecture with probability that bodies do exist. But it is a probability only, and however scrupulously I conduct my enquiries, I cannot argue from the distinct idea of physical nature which I find in my imagination to the necessary conclusion that material things exist.

Besides this image of physical nature, which is the object of geometry, I am accustomed to imagining a great many other things such as colours, sounds, tastes, pain, and so on, but none of them so distinctly. Now, as I perceive all these things much better through the senses, by means of which, and of the memory, they seem to reach the imagination, I think that, in order to consider them more conveniently, it is appropriate to consider at the same time what sensing is, and to see if from the ideas I receive through this activity of the mind which I call sensing I may derive any certain proof of the existence of material things.

First, then, I shall call back to mind all that I once held as true on the testimony of the senses, together with the grounds on which my belief was based. Next, I shall examine the reasons which made me doubt these grounds. Finally, I shall consider what I should now believe.

Now, in the first place, my senses told me that I had a head, hands, feet, and all the other members of which the body is composed – the body which I regarded as part, or even perhaps as the whole, of myself; and my senses also told me that this body was placed among a great many others with which it had various agreeable or disagreeable contacts. I observed, further, that the agreeable contacts were accompanied by a feeling of pleasure, and the disagreeable contacts by a feeling of pain. Then, besides pleasure and pain, I also felt in me hunger and thirst and other appetites as well as certain bodily inclinations towards joy and sadness, anger, and other similar passions. In the world outside me, besides the extension, shapes, and movements of bodies, I observed in these bodies hardness, warmth, and all the other qualities that belong to the sense of touch. I also observed light, colours, smells, tastes, and sounds, the variety of which gave me the means of distinguishing the sky, the earth, the sea, and in general all material things.

Now, when I consider how the ideas of all these qualities presented themselves to my mind, and how they were the only ones I perceived directly and immediately, it certainly does not seem unreasonable that I should think that I was sensing things outside my mind, material things, that is to say, from which these ideas proceeded. For my experience showed that they presented themselves to my mind without any volition on my part, so that it was impossible for me to sense any object, however much I might wish to do so, unless it was present to the organ of one of my senses, as it was in no way within my power to sense it when it was not so present.

And, because the ideas I received through my senses were much more vivid, definite, and even in their own way distinct, than of those I could make up by reflection, or than those I found imprinted on my memory, it seemed that they could not be the products of my mind, but must necessarily have been caused in it by various external things. Then, since I had no knowledge of these things except that they gave me these ideas, I could have no other thought but that they resembled the ideas of which they were the causes.

I remembered, too, that I had made use of my senses before my reason, and I recognized that the ideas I formed of myself were not as definite as those I received through my senses, and were often composed of parts of the latter, and so I easily persuaded myself that I had no idea in my mind which had not previously passed through my senses. As to the body, which I have a special right to call mine, it is not without reason that I thought it belonged to me more properly and closely than any other; for I could never be separated from it as I could from other bodies; it was in it and for it that I felt every appetite and every passion; and, again, I was affected by feelings of pleasure and pain in its parts, and not in those of other bodies separate from it.

Finally, when I considered how sadness of the spirit follows upon a sensation of pain, while joy is born of a pleasurable one, or how a certain sensation in the stomach I called hunger is followed by a desire for food, and dryness of the throat by a desire to drink, and so on, I could find no explanation of all this save in the teaching of nature, for there is certainly no affinity or relationship

that I can understand between this sensation in the
stomach and the desire to eat, any more than between the
sensing of something that causes pain and the thought
of sadness which arises from this sensation. In the same
way, I seemed to be following the teaching of nature in
my judgements about the objects of the senses, and I had
convinced myself that these judgements were right before
I had weighed the reasons which might justify them.

Thereafter, however, various experiences ruined all my
faith in the senses. For I often observed that towers that
looked round from a distance seemed square when I
approached them, and that huge statues, erected on the
summits of these towers, looked very small when I gazed
up at them from below; and so, in innumerable other
instances, I found that judgements based on the outer
senses were erroneous. And not on the outer senses only,
but on the inner senses as well. Is there, for instance, anything more intimate, more internal, than a feeling of pain?
And yet I have heard people who have had an arm or a
leg amputated say that it still seemed to them sometimes
that they felt pain in the amputated limb; and this gave
me reason to doubt whether any one of my limbs was
really affected even though I felt pain in it.

To these reasons for doubting the evidence of my
senses I have recently added two more of a very general
kind. The first is that whatever I perceived through my
senses, when awake, I could sometimes perceive in sleep,
and as I had no reason for supposing that what I perceived
in sleep was caused by external things, I did not see why
I should entertain this belief with regard to what I
perceived through my senses when awake. The second
reason was that, while I remained ignorant of the author
of my being, or while at least I feigned this ignorance, I
saw no reason why I should not have been so constituted
by nature as to be deceived even when the truth seemed
most obvious.

As for the reasons which had hitherto convinced me of the veracity of the senses, I found it easy to answer them. For, since nature fills me with impulses of which reason disapproves, I did not think I should place too much trust in the teachings of nature. True, the ideas I received through my senses do not depend upon my will, but that is no reason for concluding that they proceed from things independent of me, since there may be in me some faculty, though still unknown to me, which produces them.

But now I am beginning to know myself better and to have a clearer idea of the author of my being, and I do not think in truth that I should rashly accept all the deliverances of the senses; but I also do not think I should regard them all as doubtful.

To begin with, as I know that all the things I understand clearly and distinctly can be made by God just as I conceive them, it is enough that I can understand a particular thing clearly and distinctly by itself for me to be certain that the one is distinct or different from the other, because they can be placed in existence separately by God; nor does it matter how this separation is caused so that I may judge them to be different. Now, from the fact that I know for certain that I exist, while I am unaware of anything that belongs to my essence, or nature, except that I am a thinking thing,[1] I rightly conclude that my whole essence consists in this, that I am a thinking thing, a substance, that is to say, whose whole nature or essence consists in thinking; and, although perhaps (or rather, as I shall say further on, certainly) I have a body to which I am closely united, yet I have, on the other hand, a distinct idea of myself as purely a thinking, and not an extended thing, and, on the other, I have a distinct idea of the body as something which is extended but does not think, so that it is certain that this self of mine, this soul by which I

1. See Note on Cartesian Terminology, p. 192.

am, is wholly and really distinct from my body, and can exist without it.

Next, I find in me certain special ways of thinking, the faculties, that is, of imagining and sensing, without which I can clearly and distinctly conceive myself as existing whole and entire, but which I cannot conceive of as existing without me, without, that is to say, an intellectual substance in which they inhere. For the formal concept I have of them includes some degree of intellection, and I see that they are distinct from me as the modes of a substance are distinct from that substance itself.

I find I have other faculties as well, such as the power to change location, to adopt various postures, and so on, and these faculties, like the preceding ones, cannot be conceived except as inhering in some substance without which they cannot exist. What is evident, however, is that these faculties, if it be true that they exist, must belong to a material or extended substance, not an intellectual substance, since in the clear and distinct notion of them there is contained some sort of extension, but no intellection.

In addition to the above, I have besides a certain passive faculty of sensing, that is to say, the power of receiving and knowing the ideas of material things, but it would be useless to me unless there were in me, or elsewhere, an active power capable of forming and producing these ideas. Now this active power cannot be in me insofar as I am a thinking thing, since it does not presuppose my understanding, and because these ideas often do not present themselves to me with my co-operation; indeed they often appear against my will. This power must therefore exist in some substance different from me, which (to repeat a point I have already made) must be, formally or virtually, as real as the ideas produced are objectively so in my mind. And this substance must be a body, that is to say, a physical nature which contains formally and in fact all that the ideas contain objectively and by representation. Or else this substance is God Himself, or else some creature of a higher order than physical nature in which this reality is virtually contained.

But God does not deceive, and so it is manifest that He does not send me these ideas directly or through some creature in whom their reality is only virtually contained. For He has given me no means of knowing that this is so, but on the contrary a great propensity to believe that these ideas emanate from material things, and it would be difficult not to think that He had deceived us, if they came from any other source. It follows, consequently, that material things exist.

This does not mean, however, that they exist exactly as our senses show them to be, for perception through the senses is notably obscure and confused; but what I understand clearly and distinctly, all, that is to say, that in general constitutes the object of mathematical science, this at least is what it purports to be. As for other material things, either in particular cases, as for instance the size and shape of the sun, and so on, or in cases where the understanding lacks clarity, as with light, sound, pain, and other similar matters, even here, where all is doubt and uncertainty, since God does not deceive, He would not allow error to infest my mind without giving me the power to correct it, and so I can conclude with assurance that even in these cases I have the means to achieve the truth.

And, first, there is no doubt that whatever nature teaches us contains some truth, for by nature I now mean nothing else than God Himself, or the order established by Him among created things, as by my own nature, in particular, I mean nothing but the co-ordination of all that God has bestowed upon me. Now there is nothing that my nature teaches more expressly than that I have a body which is indisposed when I feel pain, which needs to eat or drink when I feel hungry or thirsty. Nor may I in any way doubt that there is some truth in all this. For nature also teaches me by these feelings of pain, hunger, thirst, and so on, that I am not just lodged in my body like a pilot in his ship, but that I am intimately united with it, and so confused and intermingled with it that I and my body compose, as it were, a single whole. If this were not so, I should feel no pain when my body was injured; I should simply note the injury with my understanding, as a pilot sees with his eyes any damage to his ship. And when my body needs to drink or to eat, I should simply know the fact without being informed by a confused feeling of hunger or of thirst. All these feelings of hunger, thirst, pain, and so on, are, indeed, nothing but certain confused ways of thinking, which arise from, and depend upon, the union, the intermingling, as it were, of the mind and the body.

Nature teaches me, besides, that several other bodies exist round mine, with some of which I should welcome contact, while shunning it with others. And, certainly, from the fact that I sense such a diversity of colours, smells, tastes, sounds, heat, hardness, and so on, I may well conclude that there are in the bodies, from which all these varied sensations emanate, a variety of corresponding modifications, even though these modifications may not be exactly similar to their effects. Again, from the fact that among these varied sensations I find some pleasant and others unpleasant, I can draw the certain conclusion that my body, or rather I myself, insofar as I am composed of a body and a soul, can be agreeably or disagreeably affected by the surrounding bodies.

On the other hand, there are many other things nature seems to have taught me, but which I have not acquired in this way, and which have entered my mind through a certain habit of making hasty and ill-considered judgements. There is the opinion that space is empty when I see nothing moving in it or affecting my senses; that in a warm body there is something corresponding to my idea of heat; that a white body has the very whiteness I sense; that something bitter or sweet has in fact the taste of bitterness or sweetness, and so with the other senses; that stars and towers, and all other distant objects, have the shape and size they present from afar, and so on and so forth.

In order, however, that there should be nothing in all this that I do not perceive distinctly enough, I must define precisely what I properly mean by speaking of the teaching of nature. For I speak of nature here in a more restricted sense than when I called it the co-ordination of all the faculties God has given me, since these include a good deal that concerns only the mind, with which I am not here concerned, in speaking of nature, as when I speak of knowing the truth that what has been done cannot be undone, and other similar truths which I know by the natural light of the mind, and without the instrumentality of the body. In the same way, I am not concerned with the body alone, as, for example, with its weight and so on, but only with what God has given me insofar as I am compounded of both body and mind. Now it is from this point of view that nature teaches me to avoid what gives me a sensation of pain, and to seek out what gives me some feeling of pleasure; but I do not see that, beyond this, nature teaches me to come to any conclusion regarding the existence of the external things which are the objects of our sense-perceptions, before the mind has scrupulously examined them; for it belongs to the mind alone, and not to the compound of body and mind, to know the truth in this matter.

Thus, although a star makes no more impression on my eyes than the flame of a small torch, there is in me no real or positive propensity to believe that the star is no larger than the flame; I have simply thought so since childhood without any rational grounds for my belief. And, although when I come near a fire I feel heat, or even pain, if I come too near, I have no reason to think that there is something similar to this heat, or to this pain, in the fire, but only that there is something in the fire, whatever it may be, which excites in me this feeling of heat or of pain.

In the same way, although there are portions of space in which I find nothing that excites my senses, I must not conclude thereby that these portions of space are empty. But I see what it is, I see that in these, and in many similar cases, I am accustomed to pervert and confound the natural order. These sensations, or sense-perceptions, have been bestowed upon me in order to signify to my mind which things are suitable, and which harmful, for the compound of which it is part; and for this purpose they are sufficiently clear and sufficiently distinct. But I make use of them as infallible rules for discerning the essences of external things, about which the information they provide is highly obscure and highly confused.

I have, however, already given enough consideration to the fact that error infests the judgements we make in this way, despite the sovereign goodness of God. There remains one difficulty regarding what nature teaches me to welcome or to avoid, and regarding my internal senses; for I have noticed that I am subject to error in this respect, and so that I am directly misled by my nature. Thus the agreeable taste of some poisoned food may induce me to take the poison, and so mislead me. In this case, however, nature only invites me to take the food because of its agreeable savour, and does not make me desire the poison, and my conclusion is simply that my nature does not know everything; nor is this a matter for surprise, since man having a finite nature can only have a limited knowledge.

There are cases, however, which occur frequently

enough, when we go wrong directly under the influence of nature, as when a sick man desires to drink or to eat what is bad for him. It may be argued that his nature misleads him because it is corrupted, but this does not remove the difficulty, since a sick man is no less the creature of God than a man who is well, and it is as repugnant to the goodness of God that nature should be misleading in the one case as in the other. Just as a clock composed of wheels and counterweights is as obedient to the laws of nature when it is badly made, and does not mark the hours properly, as when it fully satisfies the desire of its maker, so too, if I consider the human body to be so constructed and composed of bones, nerves, muscles, veins, blood, and flesh, that even if it were mindless, it would still move in the same way as it does now, when it moves involuntarily, without, that is to say, the help of the mind, and only through the disposition of the bodily organs, I recognize easily that it would be as natural for this body, if it were suffering, for example, from the dropsy, to suffer from dryness of the throat (which usually signifies to the mind a sensation of thirst), and to be disposed by this dryness to make those nervous and muscular movements that are required for drinking, and so increase its sickness and do itself harm, as it would be natural for this same body, when it is well, to be induced to drink for its own good by a similar dryness of the throat. And, although in respect of the use to which a clock is destined by the clockmaker it may be said to be spoilt in its nature, when it does not mark the hours properly, and although, in the same way, the human machine, when it is regarded as designed by God to execute all those movements that are proper to it, may reasonably seem not to be following the order of nature, when it has a dry throat and yet drinking is inimical to its preservation, I must avow that this way of explaining is very different from my former one. For this new explanation is but a verbal argument, entirely dependent upon my thought which has instituted a comparison between a sick man and a badly-made clock and my idea of a man who is well and a well-made clock, and extrinsic to what it signifies; whereas, by my previous explanation of nature, I mean something that is really found in things, and therefore which is not without some truth.

What remains true, nevertheless, is that, although it is pure verbalism to speak of the dropsical body being corrupted in its nature because, without needing to drink, it has an arid throat, yet in respect of the human compound, that is to say, of the mind or soul united to this body, it is not a matter of words, but a real error of nature that it should be thirsty when to drink would do it harm. I must proceed, therefore, to consider how it is that the goodness of God does not prevent human nature from being fallacious in this sense.

Now to begin my enquiry, I first observe that there is a great difference between the mind and the body in that the body is by nature always divisible, and that the mind is wholly indivisible; for, when I consider my mind, that is to say, myself insofar as I am only a thinking thing, I can distinguish no parts, but conceive myself as a single whole; and, although the whole mind seems to be united to the whole body, if the body were to lose a foot, or an arm, or some other part, it is certain that the mind would not lose anything thereby. Nor can my powers of willing, sensing, understanding, and so forth, be properly described as parts of the mind, for it is the same mind, whole and entire, that is employed in willing, sensing, understanding, and so on. But with bodies, or extended things, it is quite the contrary, for there is none I cannot dissect in thought, none that my mind cannot easily divide into several parts, and none, consequently, that it does not know to be divisible. And that would be enough to show me that the mind, or soul, of man is entirely different from the body, if I were not already sufficiently aware of the fact.

I observe, too, that the mind is not affected by all the parts of the body, but only by the brain, or even, perhaps, by that small part of the brain in which resides what is called the common sense,[1] and as this sense is affected in the same way, so it makes the mind aware of the same sensation, even though other parts of the body may be otherwise affected, as is shown by countless experiences which I need not recall.

The next point to observe is that the nature of the body is such that no part of it can be moved by some somewhat distant part without its being possible for it to be moved in the same way by any one of the intervening parts, even though the distant part is itself immobile. For example, in the tightly stretched cord, ABCD, if one happened to pull at the last part D, the first part A would not be otherwise set in motion than if one had pulled at one of the intervening parts B or C, while the last part D remained still. In the same way, when I feel pain in the foot, physics teaches me that this feeling is communicated through the nerves which are dispersed in the foot, and which, being stretched like cords from there to the brain, pluck at the part of the brain where they end, when they themselves are plucked at in the foot, thus causing a certain movement instituted by nature to make the mind aware of a pain, just as if the pain were in the foot. Because, however, these nerves have to pass through the leg, the thigh, the small of the back, the back itself, and the neck, in order to stretch from the foot to the brain, it may well happen that, while the extremities of these nerves remain untouched in the foot, the parts that pass through the small of the back or the neck are affected, causing nevertheless the same effect upon the brain as would be caused by an injury in the foot, so that the mind is compelled to feel the same pain in the foot as if it had received an injury

1. See Note on Cartesian Terminology, p. 192.

there. It is in this way that he must judge all sense-perceptions.

Finally I observe that, since each of the movements reaching that part of the brain by which the mind is immediately affected is the cause of a particular feeling, nothing better could be imagined or wished for than that, among all the feelings it is capable of causing, each movement should make the mind aware of what is most proper and most commonly useful for the preservation of the human body, when it is in good health. Now experience shows us that all the sensations nature has given us are of this kind, and thus there is nothing in any of them which does not reveal the power and goodness of God who caused them.

Thus, for example, when the nerves in the foot are strongly and more than ordinarily affected, the agitation passes through the spinal chord to the brain, causing an impression on the mind that makes it feel a pain as being located in the foot, whereby the mind itself is warned and urged to do what it can to drive away the cause of this pain as being dangerous and harmful to the foot.

It is true, of course, that God could have so constituted the nature of man that the effect upon the brain should make the mind aware of something quite different – of itself, for instance, insofar as it is connected with the brain, or the foot, or with some intervening part of the body, or, again, the impression might be something altogether different, but nothing of all this would be as useful for the preservation of the body as those sensations which are in fact brought to the attention of the mind. And so, when we need to drink, we feel a certain dryness of the throat, and the impression passes through the nerves of the throat till it reaches the inner parts of the brain, making the mind aware of a feeling of thirst, because in this event there is nothing more advantageous for us than to know that we need to drink for the preservation of our health; and the same may be said of all such occurrences.

Now from all this it follows clearly that, despite the sovereign goodness of God, man's nature, insofar as he is composed of a mind and a body, cannot but be occasionally fallacious. For suppose some cause affecting not the foot, but some section of the nerves that stretch from the foot to the brain, or even the brain itself, then the movement passing through the nerves will be the same as ordinarily occurs when the foot is injured, and pain will be felt as if it were in the foot, so that the sensation is by nature deceptive. But an identical impression on the brain cannot but produce an identical perception in the mind, and as this awareness is much more frequently caused by an injury to the foot than in some other way, it is much more reasonable that there should always be a sensation of pain in the foot than elsewhere. Similarly, although dryness of the throat does not always come, as it usually does, from the body's need to drink for the sake of its health, but sometimes from a condition of a contrary nature, as we know in the case of those afflicted with dropsy, it is much better that it should deceive in this case than that it should always do so when the body is well. And we may deal in the same way with all such difficulties.

Finally, all these considerations are of the greatest use to me, not only for taking note of the errors to which my nature is subject, but also for avoiding them, or for correcting them more easily. Knowing now that my senses are more often trustworthy than not with regard to what concerns the welfare of the body, and that I can usually employ several of them in the examination of the same object; being able, furthermore, to make use of my memory in binding together present and past knowledge, and of my understanding which has already detected all the causes of my errors, I need no longer have any apprehension of falsehood in the normal deliverances of my senses, and I must explode, as worthy only of ridicule, my hyperbolical doubts of the last few days. In particular, I may rid myself of that general incertitude about sleep, which I was unable to distinguish from my waking moments. Now I see a notable difference between them in that memory can never connect our dreams together or with the general course of our lives, as it can with what happens when we are awake; and, indeed, if someone were to appear before me all of a sudden, while I was awake, and were to disappear in the same way, like the images we see in dreams, I should regard him, not unreasonably, as a spectre, a phantom of my brain, similar to those figures which come to me in sleep, rather than as a real man. But when I perceive something of which I clearly know the provenance, the location, and the moment of time, and whose perception I can link up uninterruptedly with the rest of my life, I am fully assured that I am perceiving it, not in my sleep, but in my waking life. And so, I may not doubt the truth of anything about which, after I have appealed to my senses, my memory, and my understanding, I find no contradiction in what these faculties tell me. For God does not deceive us, and it follows necessarily, therefore, that I cannot be mistaken in such an event.

But, as the necessity for action often forces us to make up our minds before we have the leisure to submit things to a careful scrutiny, it must be admitted that the life of men is very often subject to error in particular cases, and, besides, we must recognize the weakness and infirmity of our nature.

Letter-Preface to the Principles of Philosophy

*

[*The* Principles of Philosophy *containing a general account of Descartes' metaphysical and physical theories was published in Latin in 1644. A French version appeared three years later headed by a preface in the form of a letter from Descartes to the translator. This letter-preface is of importance not as adding anything to the Cartesian doctrine, but as summing up Descartes' view of what philosophy should be, and of his own achievement as a philosopher. By this time Descartes was a European figure, and he writes with assurance, indeed with a touch of aggressiveness, in a manner very different from the* Discourse on Method, *his first published work. After the* Principles *Descartes' only major work is the* Treatise on the Passions of the Soul *published just before his death in 1650.*]

Sir,

The translation of my PRINCIPLES which you have taken the trouble to do is so clear and so accomplished a work that it will be read by more people in French than in Latin, and better understood. My only fear is that the title may discourage a number of people who have not been brought up on the humanities, or else who have acquired a poor opinion of philosophy through being dissatisfied with the kind of philosophy they have been taught; and this makes me think that it would be as well to add a preface stating the subject of the book, my intention in writing it, and the use to which it can be put. But, although it should fall to me to compose this preface, since I must know all this better than anybody else, I cannot bring myself to do more than to set down here a summary of the principal points that should be treated of in such a preface, leaving it to your discretion to decide how much of this letter should be made known to the public.

I should first have liked to explain what philosophy is, beginning with the most obvious remarks, as that the word *philosophy* signifies the study of wisdom, and that wisdom means, not only prudence in the affairs of life, but also the perfect knowledge of all that a man requires as much for the conduct of his life as for the preservation of his health, and for the progress of the arts; and, finally, that for knowledge to be thus perfect it must be deduced from first causes, so that, in studying to acquire it (and that is what is properly called philosophizing), we must begin with the search for first causes, that is to say, of principles which must satisfy two conditions: first, that they should be so clear and so evident that the human mind cannot doubt their truth, when it comes to consider them attentively; second, that the knowledge of everything else should depend upon them in such a way that while they can be known without the knowledge of other things, nothing can be known without them. The next step is to deduce from these principles as much knowledge as depends upon them, taking care that each link in the chain of deductions is itself immediately evident. Truly, only God is perfectly wise; men have more or less wisdom as they have more or less knowledge of the most important truths. Nor is there in all this anything, I believe, with which all the learned would not agree.

I should then have offered for consideration the use of philosophy, and shown that, since it extends to all that the human mind can know, it alone distinguishes us from savages and barbarians, each nation being the more civilized and polished as its citizens are the better versed in philosophy. It would follow that the greatest good for a state is to have true philosophers, and, further, that for each man in particular it is not only useful to live among those who engage in this study, but incomparably better to engage in it himself, just as it is doubtless better to make use of one's own eyes to guide oneself and enjoy the beauties of colour and light than to keep them closed and to rely upon the guidance of another. Even this, however, is better than keeping them closed and guiding oneself. For, to try to live without philosophizing is, properly speaking, to keep one's eyes closed without ever trying to open them, while the pleasure we get from seeing what our sight reveals to us is as nothing compared with the contentment that arises from the knowledge of all that philosophy shows us. Finally, the study of philosophy is of more use in regulating our behaviour and ordering our lives than our eyes are of use in guiding our steps. Brute beasts, who have nothing but their bodies to preserve, are in constant search of food; but men, whose chief possession is their minds, should employ themselves chiefly in the search for wisdom, which is the true nourishment of the mind; and I am sure that there are many who would not fail to do so, if they had any hope of succeeding and knew how much it lay within their capacity. There is no soul so lowly, so much attached to the objects of the senses, that it does not sometimes wish for some higher good, even though it does not know in what that higher good consists. Those who are most favoured by fortune, and have an abundance of health, wealth, and honours, are no more free of this desire than the others; on the contrary, I believe they yearn more ardently after some other good, some good of a sovereign nature much higher than the goods they possess. Now this sovereign good, considered from the point of view of the natural reason, without the light of supernatural faith, is nothing but the knowledge of truth by its first causes, that is to say, wisdom, of which philosophy is the study. And, as all that philosophy teaches is wholly true, it has only got to be properly deduced to convince.

What hinders this conviction, however, is the fact that those who profess to be philosophers[1] are often less wise and less reasonable than those who have never applied themselves to this study; and so I should then have given a summary of what constitutes our knowledge, and of the degrees of wisdom we have reached. The first degree

1. The Scholastics.

contains only those notions which are so clear of themselves that they can be acquired without meditation; the
second includes all the knowledge we acquire from
experience and through the senses; the third covers what
we learn from our intercourse with other men; and to
these may be added a fourth, the reading of books – not
of all books, but particularly of those written by people
capable of instructing us, for the reading of such books
is a sort of conversation with their authors. And it seems
to me that the wisdom we commonly have is acquired by
these four means. For Revelation is not here in question,
as it does not lead us on step by step, but raises us suddenly
to the heights of infallible faith. Now there have been, at
all times, great men whose object it has been to find a
fifth degree of wisdom, incomparably higher and more
assured than the other four: that is, the discovery of the
first causes and true principles from which may be deduced the reasons of everything that can be known; and
it is chiefly those who have made this effort who are called
philosophers. I do not know, however, that any one of
them has so far succeeded in this search. The first and the
chief among those whose writings we possess are Plato
and Aristotle, between whom there is no difference save
that the former, following in the steps of his master,
Socrates, confessed ingenuously that he had been unable
to find anything certain, and was content to state what
seemed like the truth, inventing certain principles to this
effect on which to base his reasoning; whereas Aristotle,
with less frankness, although he had been Plato's disciple
for twenty years, entirely changed the way of teaching
these principles, and proposed them as true and certain,
although there is nothing to show that Plato ever regarded them as such. Now these two men had a great
deal of intelligence, and a great deal of the wisdom
acquired in the four ways I have described, and this gave
them so much authority that those who came after them

were more concerned with following their opinions than with finding something better. Between these two groups of disciples the principal divergence of opinion was on the question as to whether there should be a general doubt of everything, or whether some things were certain. And this quarrel led, on both sides, to extravagant errors. Some of the partisans of doubt extended it even to our everyday actions, and neglected the use of prudence in their behaviour; the partisans of certainty supposed that it depended upon the senses in which they placed all their trust, so that Epicurus, it is said, went to the point of daring to affirm that the sun was no bigger than it appeared to be, despite all the arguments of the astronomers. And this defect is to be observed in most disputes, namely, that, as the truth lies in the middle between the two conflicting opinions, each one departs the further from it the greater his passion for debate.

However, the error of those who inclined too much to the side of doubt was not long followed, and that of their opponents has been partially corrected by the recognition that the senses deceive us about many things. Nevertheless, it does not appear that the latter error has been entirely cleared away by its being shown that certainty is not of the senses, but of the understanding, when the mind perceives something evident, and that, as long as our knowledge belongs to the first four degrees of wisdom, we should not doubt what seems true for our everyday behaviour, but we should not hold it with such certainty that we cannot change our minds when obliged to do so by the evidence. For lack of knowing this truth, or else, if some have known it, for lack of using it, most of those who have wished to be philosophers[1] during these last centuries have blindly followed Aristotle, often corrupting the sense of his writing by attributing various opinions to him which he would not recognize as his

1. The Scholastics.

own, if he came back into this world; while those who have not followed him (and some of the best minds are among them) have yet been so imbued with his opinions in their youth (since those are the only ones taught in our schools) that their minds have been too clouded with prejudice to attain to the knowledge of the true principles. And though I esteem them all, and do not wish to incur the odium of finding fault with them, I can give one proof of what I say which none of them will, I think, refuse to accept, and that is, that they have all taken as a principle of explanation something they have not perfectly understood. For example, I know none of these philosophers who has not supposed that heaviness was a property of terrestrial bodies, but, although experience shows very clearly that bodies called heavy descend towards the centre of the earth, we do not know for all that what the nature is of what is called heaviness, we know nothing, that is to say, of the cause or principle which makes these bodies descend in this way, and we must learn about it from elsewhere. The same may be said of a void, of atoms, of what is called hot, or cold, dry, or wet, of salt, of sulphur, and of mercury, and of all such things which some have taken as principles of explanation. But all the conclusions drawn from a principle that is not evident cannot themselves be evident, even though the deduction is evident. It follows that all the reasonings they have based on such principles do not give the certain knowledge of anything at all, nor lead them, consequently, one step forward in the search for wisdom. Even if they have chanced upon a particular truth, it has only been by some of the four means deduced above.

However, I have no wish to lessen the eminence to which each one of them may pretend. I simply feel obliged to say, for the consolation of the unlearned, that, just as the traveller who turns his back on his destination leaves it the further behind the faster and longer he walks, so that even though he is brought back to the right road he cannot arrive as quickly as if he had not been walking at all, so the wrong principles lead one further away from the knowledge of truth and wisdom the more one cultivates them, and the greater care one devotes to drawing out their various consequences, in the belief that one is philosophizing in the right way. The conclusion is that those who have learned the least of what has hitherto been called philosophy are the most capable of learning the true one.

After I had made all this quite clear, I should have liked to set forth, at this point, the reasons that serve to show that the true principles, by which one reaches that highest degree of wisdom which is the sovereign good of human life, are those I have put into this book; and only two reasons are required to prove my point, the first being that they are very clear, and the second, that everything else can be deduced from them; for these are the only two conditions required. Now I find it easy to prove their clarity. In the first place, there is the manner in which I found them, that is to say, by rejecting everything in which I found the slightest suspicion of a doubt; for it is certain that what cannot be rejected in this way is, when attentively considered, what is clearest and most evident to the human mind. Thus, by reflecting that anyone who wishes to doubt everything cannot, in doubting, doubt his own existence, and that the entity which reasons in this way, being unable to doubt that it exists, while doubtful nevertheless of everything else, is not what we call the body but what we call the soul or thought, I took the being or existence of this thought for my first principle, from which I very clearly deduced that there is a God, the Author of everything in the world, who, being the source of all truth, has not created our understanding of such a nature that it can go wrong when we pass judgement on what we very clearly and distinctly perceive. These are all the principles of which I make use regarding what is immaterial or metaphysical; and from them I deduce very clearly the principles of what is corporeal or physical, namely, that there are bodies, having extension in length, breadth, and depth, which have sundry shapes, and move in various ways.

The second reason that proves the clarity of my principles is that they have been known at all times, and even accepted as true and indubitable by all men, except that the existence of God has been doubted by some, because they attribute too much authority to their senses and God can neither be seen nor touched. However, although the truths I count among my principles have been known at all times and by all men, no one, to my knowledge, has so far recognized them as the principles of philosophy from which the knowledge of everything else in the world can be deduced. I have, therefore, to prove that they are such, and it seems to me that I cannot do it better than by experience, that is to say, by inviting my public to read my book. For, although I have not dealt with everything in it, as it would have been impossible to do so, what I have had occasion to deal with I think I have so explained that those who read with care will have reason to be convinced that there is no need to look for other principles than those I have set forth in order to reach the summit of human knowledge – especially if, after having read my writings, they consider the diversity of matters explained in them, and if, after perusing the works of others, they see the weakness of their reasoning on the same subjects with the help of principles different from mine. Finally, I could have said, to ease the task for my readers, that those who are imbued with my principles have less trouble in understanding the writings of others, and in knowing their exact value, than those who are not so imbued. It is the contrary of what I said above about those who have begun with the ancient philosophy, and who, the more they have studied it, are thereby the less fitted to learn the new one.

I should also have added a word of advice as to how my book should be read. I should like the reader first to go through it as a whole, as he might do with a romance, without too much forcing of his attention, and without stopping at the difficulties he might meet with, so as to begin only with a general notion of the subjects dealt with. Then, if he finds that these matters deserve further examination, or if he has the curiosity to enquire into the causal explanations, he can read the book a second time in order to follow the course of my argument. Nor should he feel suddenly rebuffed, if he cannot follow it everywhere, or if he cannot understand it in all its details. All he needs to do is to mark the passages in which difficulties arise, and to continue uninterruptedly to the end. A third reading will, I venture to think, solve most of the difficulties previously noted; if some remain, he will discover their solution in the end by taking up the book again.

I have observed in examining the natural ability of many people that there is hardly anyone so heavy and tardy in mind as to be unable to enter into the right disposition, and even to reach the heights of knowledge, provided he has conducted his thoughts in the right way. And this may be proved by reason; for, since the principles are clear in themselves, and nothing should be deduced from them save by evident reasoning, a man always has enough intelligence to understand what follows from these principles. But, besides the hindrance of prejudices, from which no one is exempt, even though they do the most harm to those who are most versed in erroneous forms of knowledge, it is almost always the case that people of moderate ability neglect the search for knowledge because they believe themselves incapable of it, while the more eager press on too fast. The result is that they often accept doubtful principles from which they draw uncertain conclusions. That is why I should like to assure all those who have too little confidence in their own powers that there is nothing in my writings which they cannot fully understand, if they take the trouble to study them, while warning the others that even the best minds will need to give a good deal of time and attention, if they are to take heed of all I have intended to include in my work.

After that, and in order that my aim in publishing my work should be properly understood, I should like to explain here the order to be followed in instructing oneself. First of all, a man who has only the ordinary and imperfect knowledge which can be acquired by the four means I have discussed above, must above all strive to formulate for himself a moral code that may suffice to govern his everyday behaviour, which allows of no delay as our first task is to live well. Next, he must study logic: not the logic of the Schoolmen,[1] which is, properly speaking, nothing but a kind of dialectics, which teaches us how to make others understand what we know already, or even how to utter unconsidered opinions on subjects about which we know nothing, and which consequently corrupts our good sense rather than increases it; but the logic which teaches the proper conduct of the reason is the discovery of the truths of which we have been ignorant; and, as logic, in this sense, depends largely upon practice, it is right to exercise it assiduously on the rules that apply to easy and simple problems, like those of mathematics. Lastly, when a man has acquired a certain knack in finding the truth in these matters, he should begin, once and for all, to apply himself to the study of true philosophy, of which the first part is metaphysics, comprising the first principles of knowledge which include the explanation of the principal attributes

1. The Scholastics.

of God, of the immateriality of the soul, and of all those clear and simple notions that inhabit our minds. The second part of philosophy is physics in which, after having discovered the true principles of material things, we examine generally how the whole universe is composed, and in particular the nature of the earth and of all that is common to it, such as air, water, fire, the lodestone, and other minerals. Following this, we need also to examine the nature of plants, of animals, and above all of man, so that we may be able thereafter to discover the other sciences which are useful to him. Thus the whole of philosophy is like a tree, of which metaphysics forms the roots and physics the trunk, while the branches which grow from this trunk constitute all the other sciences which may be reduced to three: medicine, mechanics, and ethics – I mean the highest and most perfect form of ethics which, as it presupposes a complete knowledge of the other sciences, is the last degree of wisdom.

Now, as it is not from the roots, nor from the trunk of a tree, that we pluck the fruit, but from the extremities of its branches, so the principal uses of philosophy derive from those parts of it which we learn the last. But, although I am almost entirely ignorant of them, the zeal I have always felt for the service of the public led me to publish, ten or twelve years ago, some essays on certain subjects which I thought I had mastered. The introduction to these essays was a discourse on the method of properly conducting one's reason and of seeking the truth in the sciences, in which I summarized the main rules of logic, and of an imperfect code of morals that could be provisionally followed as long as one was ignorant of a better one. The remaining parts consisted of three treatises, the first on Dioptrics, the next on Meteors, and the last on Geometry. The essay on Dioptrics was designed to show that one can go far enough in philosophy to attain, by this means, to a knowledge of the arts that serve humanity, since the invention of the microscope is one of the most difficult that has ever been sought after. By the essay on Meteors I hoped to secure recognition of the difference there is between philosophy as I have cultivated it and philosophy as it is taught in the Schools, where it is also the custom to treat of Meteors. In the essay on Geometry, I claimed to demonstrate various truths I had discovered, which were previously unknown, so as to encourage all men in the search for truth. Later on, foreseeing that many would have difficulty in grasping the foundations of metaphysics, I sought to explain the principles in a book of MEDITATIONS, which is not very long, but of which the volume has been enlarged, and the subject-matter much illumined, by the objections sent to me by many very learned persons, and by my own replies to these objections.[1] Finally, when it seemed to me that my previous work had prepared the minds of my readers to receive the principles of philosophy, I also published these, dividing the work into four parts, of which the first contained the principles of knowledge, which is what can be called first philosophy or metaphysics; and that is why, in order fully to understand this first part, it is proper to begin with my Meditations on the same subject. The three other parts contain everything of the most general order in physics, that is, the explanation of the general laws or principles of nature, and the way in which the heavens, the fixed stars, the planets, the comets, and in general the whole universe, is disposed; then, in particular, the nature of this earth, and of air, water, fire, and the lodestone, which bodies are most commonly found in relation to it; and so all the qualities observed in these bodies, such as light, heat, weight, and so on. In this way, I think I have begun to expound the whole of philosophy without ever omit-

1. These Objections and Replies have been omitted from this translation for reasons of space.

ting any of the considerations which should precede those that come at a later stage.

However, if I am to carry my design to its conclusion, I must explain in the same way the nature of the more individual bodies that cover the earth – minerals, plants, animals, and in particular man; finally, I should give an exact account of medicine, ethics, and mechanics. That, I say, is what I should do in order to provide mankind with a whole body of philosophical knowledge; and I do not yet feel so old, so lacking in confidence in my own powers, or so far removed from the knowledge of all that remains to be known, that I would not dare to undertake the accomplishment of this design, if I had the means to conduct all those experiments I should need in order to sustain and justify my reasonings. But, as I see that this needs considerable expenditure, beyond the capacity of a private individual unaided by the public, and as I do not see any likelihood of such assistance, I think that I should now content myself with pursuing my studies for my own instruction, and that posterity will forgive me if I cease to work for its benefit.

Nevertheless, in order to show how I think I have already served posterity, I shall here set down the fruits of my principles, as I conceive them to be. The first is the satisfaction of discovering many truths hitherto unknown; for, although the truth very often excites the imagination less than error and pretence because it seems simpler and less wonderful, yet the contentment it gives is always more lasting and more solid. The second is that the study of these principles accustoms us, little by little, to judging more correctly of what we encounter, and so makes us wiser, while our usual philosophy has the contrary effect; for it is easy to observe how those whom we called pedants are rendered less capable of reason by this philosophy than they would be if they had never acquired it. The third fruit is that the truth of these principles being at once very clear and very simple, they will remove all subjects of dispute, and so dispose the minds of men to gentleness and concord; whereas, on the contrary, the disputations in the Schools,[1] as they imperceptibly render those who practise them more susceptible and more obstinate, are perhaps the first cause of those heresies and dissensions which now agitate the world. Last and chief among the fruits of my principles is that one can, by cultivating them, discover many truths I have not touched upon; and so, passing little by little from one to the other, one may acquire in time a perfect knowledge of the whole of philosophy and rise to the very summit of wisdom. We see in all the arts how, although they begin by being crude and unfinished, they nevertheless reach perfection by use, because they have something true about them of which experience shows the effect. So, when we have the right principles in philosophy, we cannot fail, when we follow them, to come upon other truths sometimes. And we cannot better demonstrate the falseness of Aristotle's principles than by pointing out how they have been followed for several centuries without causing any progress in knowledge.

I know, of course, that there are some who work so hastily, and without circumspection, that though they build upon solid foundations, they never build anything safe and certain; and, as they are always the most prompt to write books, they could in a very short while undo all I have done, and introduce doubt and uncertainty into my way of philosophizing, from which I have sedulously tried to banish them. I have had an example of this quite recently in the case of someone who was most generally thought to be a follower of mine, and of whom I had even written somewhere 'that I was so sure of his mind that I did not think he had a single opinion that I should not have admitted to be my own'. But last year he published

1. Among the Scholastics, at the Sorbonne, for example.

a book, entitled *Fundamenta Physics*, in which, although he appears to have included nothing on physics or medicine which he has not derived from my writings, either from those already published, or from a still imperfect manuscript on the nature of animals which happened to fall into his hands, yet, because he has transcribed things wrongly, altered the order of exposition, and denied some metaphysical truths on which the whole of physics depends, I am obliged to disavow his work completely, and here beg my readers never to attribute to me any opinion they do not find expressly in my writings, and to accept none as true, whether they find it in my writings or elsewhere, unless they very clearly see it to be deduced from true principles.

I know also that many centuries can go by before all the truths that can be deduced from these principles have been so derived, since most of them depend upon individual experiments which will not be encountered by chance, but must be sought after, with care and expense, by men of high intelligence. Moreover, it will be difficult to find combined in the same people the skill to make use of these experiments with the resources needed to make them, while most of the best minds have conceived so bad an opinion of philosophy, because of the defects they have observed in the philosophy hitherto in use, that they will be unable to apply themselves to the task of finding a better one. However, they will see the difference between my principles and those of others, together with the grand chain of truths that can be deduced from them, and, if this makes them understand how important it is to continue in the pursuit of these truths, and to what a degree of wisdom, human perfection, and happiness, they can lead, I dare believe that there will not be one of them who will not endeavour to engage in so profitable a study, or who will not at least favour and wish to assist those who pursue it with success. May posterity gather in the harvest.

Appendix

*

A Note on Cartesian Terminology

DESCARTES is the most lucid of philosophers, but, like all philosophers he has his own vocabulary which needs to be understood. Many of the notions Descartes uses for his own purposes are, as has already been said in the Introduction, drawn from the Scholastic philosophy he was intent to destroy; he uses, in fact, the philosophical language of his day. But the philosophical language of the eighteenth century is not ours, and a few remarks on terminology may be of assistance to the modern reader.

Perfection. The meaning of this term as used by Descartes is not easy to grasp, and one is tempted to suggest that the best way to do so is to begin by forgetting its modern usage in which the word tends to mean something like 'the best ever' or 'the best possible'. Such a suggestion would, however, be at least partially misleading, for we have only to reflect upon the root meaning of the term (*perfectum* in Latin means 'complete') to see that when we call a thing perfect, in the proper sense of the word, we mean that it is complete in the sense that it is fully and truly itself. From this two things follow: in the first place, perfection is synonymous with reality insofar as the perfection of a being is its completion so that it becomes wholly and really itself; secondly, in what we may call its pure sense, the term perfection is properly applicable to God alone; all creatures are relatively imperfect and unreal. Finally, we can speak of a perfection in much the same way as we speak of an essential quality or attribute, as when we speak of God's omnipotence or His omniscience as being among His perfections, since they help to make Him really God, just as the reason and the will are perfections, in their degree, of the human being, since they are essential to humanity. Descartes' ontological proof of the existence of God can hardly be understood unless we see – as many of his critics have not – that for him perfection means reality or being.

Infinite and finite. Descartes distinguishes between infinite and finite being in the same way as the Scholastics. God is infinite because He has, or rather, is, being without limits, being in the fullest possible sense of the word; everything else, including man, is finite because it is relatively lacking in being, relatively imperfect and unreal (as has already been said); it has some touch of nothingness about it. Man, says, Descartes in a striking phrase, is poised between being and nothingness.

Formal being and Objective being. Following the later Scholastics, Descartes distinguishes between being in the ordinary sense of existence, the being, for example, of a man or a tree, called formal or actual being, and objective or representational being, the existence of ideas in the mind. The word objective is significant. For Descartes what the mind knows are its own ideas which exist in the mind as the objects of thought. This is the only meaning of 'object' in the language of Descartes, so that for him the expressions 'external object' or 'physical object' would be self-contradictory; we must speak of external, or physical, or material 'things'. The objective being of an idea corresponds to the formal being of the thing it represents. True objectivity belongs to clear and distinct ideas; the ideas of secondary qualities, being confused and obscure, have hardly any objectivity, that is to say, they are not, in modern parlance, to be taken as properly representative. The idea of God, on the other hand, is the most objective of all.

Thing. The word *thing* (Fr. *chose*, Lat. *res*) is often used by Descartes in a philosophical sense as the equivalent of the more learned term *substance*. We all know, he says, what we mean by a *thing*, that is, we all know what we mean by a *substance* – that which subsists of itself, so that a stone is a substance, but not a colour. Thus man is defined by Descartes as a *thinking thing*, or a *substance whose whole essence or nature consists in thinking*.

Sense. By *good sense* Descartes means the reason, as is clear from the first page of the *Discourse on Method*; by *the common sense* he means something quite different. This is the *sensus communis* postulated by the Scholastics, which, they argued, receives and coordinates all our sensations, internal or external. It is connected, according to Descartes, with the pineal gland.